The SUCCESS REBELLION

The SUCCESS REBELLION

Begin Creating the Life You Were Born to Live

RYAN JACKSON

Cover and Text design by Jess Morphew

In loving memory of Colm Whitty

Sep 1976 – Mar 2020

"Your life is your message to the world, make sure it's inspiring"

– Lorrin L. Lee

CONTENTS

INTRODUCTION

I grew up in East London in a single parent family with little money to spare. It was just my mum and me. Amongst my peers, it was uncommon for two parents to be together, so I accepted my situation as being the norm. It wasn't until much later in life that I realised a wholly different family dynamic existed elsewhere, with totally different approaches to family life. Despite this I didn't see myself as someone from a poor or underprivileged background, and I never really have, as on my travels I saw what real poverty looks like. However, we were definitely disadvantaged, not only from an income perspective but also from not having access to the knowledge and resources that can help overcome life's challenges.

I enjoyed school, and it served its purpose, although I was easily distracted and left without the grades I was capable of. I attended college not having a clue what I wanted to do. To be expected to make such a decision at such a young age without the 'correct' guidance and support is ridiculous. Many adults still haven't a clue what they want to do in life, so how can such responsibility be placed upon children? After struggling through the first year, I dropped out. I was bored, disengaged and was getting nothing from it.

Once I left, I lacked direction. There's no other way to say it, I became a bum, smoking weed every day, staying up all night and sleeping until noon. My life became a daily repeat of this monotonous existence. My mum threatened to throw me out every other day, and, on a couple of occasions she did, throwing my clothes on to the street. She wanted me to get a job. Not the right job . . . just any job. In a way this was my first rebellion but it was definitely not a success. I was simply a rebel without a cause.

I was against taking the conventional route, as there was nothing that was particularly attractive about the options that were on offer such as zero- hour contract jobs packing shelves or hard physical graft manual labour via an agency. Deep down I knew I had more to offer the world; I just didn't know how to begin making those steps, and I didn't have anyone to give me guidance and push me towards realising my potential. And then fate stepped in and life changed when my half-brother threw me a lifeline by getting me a job in a health club in the city.

A whole new world opened up to me with a new set of people who were living rich and varied lives, beyond what I knew or had ever experienced. Suddenly, I connected with different people.

This was the kick-start to my transformation! Having changed my environment, I was able to establish a new prospective, move beyond the lack of opportunity of my environment and at last have the chance to shine.

It broadened my horizons, providing an environment that allowed me to uncover my previously hidden natural talents. I adopted a new way of thinking, inspired by the people I was meeting; their success was contagious, and I was pulled in a new direction.

Within eighteen months of starting work as a receptionist at the health club I was the youngest and highest paid operations manager in the district. The environment, coupled with my natural skill set and my newfound belief, enabled me to thrive

I knew that I had a strong business sense, and although I hadn't set up my own business, I was running a business operation. I was responsible for the employees, increasing revenue and meeting targets. I knew I could make a success of running a business for myself. I just needed to create one, but I didn't yet know how.

On the train commuting to and from the health club I began reading, which was unusual for someone in my social group. It felt quite normal even though I had never read a book of my own volition outside of school.

The first book I bought was *Killing Pablo* by Mark Bowden, and although a surprising source of inspiration, this book changed my life. The first chapter gives an introduction to Pablo Escobar's earliest years, revealing how he came from nothing and how throughout his childhood his family experienced extreme poverty, with his mother forced to steal in order to clothe him and his siblings. And that as a teenager, Pablo fell into crime, involving himself in petty crime, such as stealing cars and robbing people and smuggling electronic goods, but whatever he did – and however illegal it was – his set up was always well thought out and beyond what his peers were doing.

He then discovered he could make a massive amount of money selling cocaine. And while he is far from a positive role model, I was impressed to read that at his peak Pablo was one of the wealthiest people on the planet, with *Forbes* magazine listing him as the fifth richest man in the world. Pablo initially studied political science at university, as his goal was to become a politician with dreams of becoming president, but I guess he realised that his ambitions could not be achieved by taking this conventional route, and so he moved to criminality to achieve his wealth and ambitions. It was his background that limited his options for success, and he chose an illegal route, but it was his drive and determination that brought him the success, and so I believe that irrespective of the commodity he was selling, he would always have achieved success.

His story planted the seed of what was possible for me and spurred me to become more than I was. It was one of those pivotal moments – a life-changing shift had occurred in me, because despite the circumstances he was born into, without following through with his education and very few resources he was still able to make his stamp on the world. Albeit through negative means, but if he could achieve that level of success in his chosen field, then with the intelligence I sensed I possessed I too could create a life far greater than what I had. Before Pablo, I had always seen success as something that you were either born into or you just had to be extremely lucky to achieve. I now understood that anyone could obtain success and to a magnitude of any scale. The penny had dropped and triggered my personal development journey.

I started to fall in love with learning, reading self-help books like *Unlimited Power* by Tony Robbins.

What I began to realise is that the system we are born in doesn't encourage an average Joe like me to succeed. It feeds and enables those on the very top. And everyone else has to conform and help drive that system forward. We slot into a particular position, and mostly we can't see beyond where we are – the level we are born into – because everyone around us is in the same place. So we accept our circumstances and our place in life as just 'how things are'.

I asked myself, how can it be right that we are born with everything we need, and yet we land in a society that teaches us limitation from the very first day of school?

I don't know how to describe it, I just had a powerful knowing in me, a strong feeling that I could do more and be more. I just had to figure out how.

I was climbing the ladder, but my expectations were growing every day. Even though I was doing well in comparison to where I started out, I knew that I was still at the bottom of the food chain, and I wanted more.

Yes, I'd had some success, but I was still immature and of a limited mindset. I still mistakenly thought that success was all about money. And what money could bring, such as all the material things in life, as well as respect, attention and even women. So began my next rebellion, though not quite a Success Rebellion. I left the health club without a roadmap or a clear vision or understanding of my true values.

I first went to work in property with a friend, but that didn't work out, so I jumped ship. I was pulled in completely the wrong direction and very nearly bought into the illusion that the road (streets) was the only way I could achieve my goals, my idea of success at that time. But I knew that there was no longevity in that world, and with seeing people I knew being sent to prison, it was pretty clear that travelling that path could only ever lead to bad outcomes. I'd arrived at a crossroad and had to decide what sort of person I wanted to be, knowing that my decision would define the rest of my life. I knew I had so much more to offer the world, but I just needed to find a way to apply it.

Despite the temptations of the easy rewards of that life, deep down I knew that wasn't the right path for me, and so I opted for a better choice. Given my background and a lack of mentoring and guidance, this wasn't going to be easy, but it had to be done. My real Success Rebellion began, and there was a lot of work to do, both real work, as well as the work I needed to do on myself, on the way I thought and behaved. Any doubts I might have had about that decision to tread the harder route faded away when one night after leaving a nightclub drunk in the early hours of the morning a close friend turned to me and said, 'Jacko, I don't know why you're wasting time with this business ting, you know you're never going to make the same money you could on the road'. Now, I love this guy, but there is no question that his doubting statement was one of the early drivers that spurred me on to make my business work! And funnily enough, a lot of my friends from that circle have now taken a similar path, as they've now seen that there is another way.

After a few failed attempts and a significant number of years travelling the wrong path, I founded Gemini Parking Solutions, which marked the true beginning of my true Success Rebellion. It has taken me on a journey of personal growth and spiritual transformation that has enabled me to step forward as the creator of a remarkable life that many could only dream of. Although I am considered an entrepreneur, when all is said and done, I'm simply a creator of the world I want to live in. I have built and grown Gemini Parking Solutions to become the UK's first leading values-based operator, raising quality to unprecedented heights, achieving recognition both from within and outside of the industry. Gemini is truly paving the way for a new era of business that focuses on its social and environmental responsibilities, as opposed to just simply accumulating profits.

Gemini's growth has, in many ways, mirrored my own, with personal development playing a crucial role in the success. I looked at how those I admired achieved their successes and began implementing their techniques. I also studied the great transformational leaders of our time to learn how to make the correct advances in my life. In short, I committed myself to attaining success and building my business day-by-day, year-by-year. With the success of Gemini, I longed to express my full potential through other business interests both here in the UK and abroad. Being a creator is about expression, and so I have now found entrepreneurship as my medium to do so.

Why is This Book Needed?

I wrote this book because I want to step forward and share what I've learned and help others to throw off the limits of their environment and transform their lives according to what they desire. I have come from nothing to create a life that I could never have dreamed of, and the crazy thing is I feel that I've only just started. I now want to give something back by helping anyone who feels that success isn't possible for them. This book will show otherwise, giving a new point of reference and set of principles to follow to realise that it is possible. I want them to discover their full potential, and to tap into their genius that lies buried within, to discover their own amazing path in life. To help them embark on their own Success Rebellion.

Who Is This Book For?

It is for anyone who has a feeling that there is more in life, but who doesn't yet know what it is.

It is also for anyone who knows they want to succeed but doesn't know how to do it. We often hear of people who achieve success but once found become their own worst enemy. Many say that to be successful you have to make a lot of sacrifices. Well, I believe that it is possible to achieve balance by getting a better understanding of who you are, of your purpose in this world, and I want people to experience true success and have fulfilment and happiness in all areas of their life.

What Are the Steps to Your Personal Success Rebellion?

First we need to remove or see through what is holding us back, and then we need to take the right action. I have developed eight key Success Rebellion principles to lead you to the life you want to live:

1. **Self-Governance** – how to take back control of your life
2. **Environment** – changing your environment to fulfil your goals
3. **Discovering Your Path** – recognising what you are here to do
4. **Vision** – the importance of having a vision for your future
5. **Values** – how to identify what is important in your life
6. **Beliefs** – how to break the barriers that hold you back from success
7. **Connection** – finding true connection with nature, others and the spirit
8. **The Power of the Plan** – set the plan for the road ahead

Every chapter dives deeply into each principle, setting out the impact on your life and laying out what changes you need to make to move towards the life you want to lead. Along the way, I'll share aspects of my own Success Rebellion journey. I'll show how I have actively used and incorporated these success principles into my daily life. You'll find questions at the end of each chapter to reflect on and help you consolidate your thinking about the Success Rebellion principle you've read about before you move on to the next chapter and reflect on how your mindset has changed as a result of what you've just read and what action you might take next.

I hope that everyone who reads this book will gain the inspiration and insights they need to start their Success Rebellion journey towards the life they want to lead.

CHAPTER I

Self-Governance

We are born into this life fully equipped with everything we need to excel and thrive. As human beings, we are perfectly designed and created to do much more than merely survive.

Any notion that we may have of settling for what we have and not doing more, is contrary to the human drive to create and build and explore. From the dawn of creation until today, this is how it's been; however, you may find that when you look at your own life or those around you, you witness a far different reality.

Our biological make-up determines our every thought, feeling and behaviour. And we are engineered to overcome challenges and dangers. From historic times, when predators and warriors were more abundant, our flight, fight or freeze responses have been hard-wired into our neurology. We have a natural ability to sense danger and the ingenuity to navigate our own way out of problems. Yet in today's world, when faced with danger or difficulty, many of us have weakened or even severed the link between ourselves and our innate gifts. Instead we have formed a dependency upon others to help us escape an unwanted reality rather than looking inside and reconnecting with the qualities that lie dormant within us, so as to better our life or circumstances.

We have surrendered our individual power under the false pretence that it serves a greater good. We have been sold a myth that placing our sovereignty in the hands of a few will offer us a better quality of life. I know this couldn't be further from the truth. For instance, we place blind trust into the hands of others, accepting their narrative as truth without carrying out our own due diligence.

How many stories have you heard from people that as children were told by their teachers or coaches that they would never amount to anything and then go on to achieve huge success?

How many reports do we hear of cases involving individuals diagnosed with incurable illness only to then seek alternative health practices elsewhere and be cured of their ailments?

Power serves those who hold it. By relinquishing your power, you surrender your soul and the eternal energy source that drives you towards the life you deserve. We are creators, and the ability to self-govern our own lives is what sets us on the path to creating a true Success Rebellion. You must accept your responsibility as a steward of your OWN life, embracing the fact that you ultimately decide what you do and do not experience.

Beyond the circumstances of your birth, your current reality is a result of the choices and actions you've taken. And for you to move towards creating a new reality, you must first wake up to the fact that the onus is upon you to create that new reality. You have to take charge and start to create new patterns of behaviour that will bring about new results, and so start the wheel of internal change that is necessary for you to step into your true power.

Loss of Governance

There are many reasons why we lose connection with our true power, but ultimately the root cause points back to a loss of self-governance and the inability to take responsibility for our own lives. As simple as this may sound, millions, if not billions of people around the world lack the ability to truly govern their lives without looking for the direction or guidance of another. I see people struggling to make a decision on the smallest of levels. In the supermarket I've witnessed friends ponder for over five minutes on what cut of chicken they should place in their shopping basket. As trivial as it may seem, it represents so much more of what is going on within their inner dialogue and is symptomatic of our society today. Being unable to identify what they want demonstrates a disconnection between them and their natural instincts. If you are unable to act upon what you want on such a micro-level without doubting your decision, how will you cope when making real decisions that will have a greater impact on your life? It's likely that you won't! And so the problem begins . . .

The Impact of Losing Sovereignty

A lack of self-governance will only lead you to a loss of sovereignty and a feeling of no control. You risk falling into a state of helplessness, becoming a victim of circumstance unable to see beyond the cards you've been dealt. Without true dominion and recall of your divine power you become exposed to the negative elements of life. Cracks, shortly followed by unhappiness, start to appear and begin to manifest themselves across all areas of our lives – our work, relationships, finances, education and our health. Here's how:

WORK

Because of a loss of sovereignty, you may feel as though you are not heard and that your voice is irrelevant. You've probably experienced times when you've felt that your contribution was undervalued and your opinion was insignificant. You feel that there is no appreciation of the role you play in the organisation. You give all you can and work beyond what is expected, but you get nothing in return. Despite your frustrations, this loss of sovereignty comes to a point when you accept this reality. You settle for less than what you deserve. You accept it for what it is. It is you who determines your worth, and by staying in a role where you are undervalued, you become the cause of your sadness.

RELATIONSHIPS

Many people feel incomplete without 'their other half', being totally displaced when their relationship breaks up. They are lost and struggle to survive alone. They have placed so much reliance emotionally, psychologically and financially upon their ex-partner, that without them in their lives, they feel empty. The cause is not the breakup but because when they got into the relationship they gave up their sovereignty and control over their own lives, becoming reliant upon and making someone else responsible for their happiness.

Happiness starts with us. Our partner should complement our happiness. That to me is self-governance – being able to regulate your own happiness and not depend upon another to bring you that happiness. We are responsible for our own emotions, and yet we look outside ourselves for other people to feed us this. And when we do, we give away our sovereignty. We place it in the hands of another and make them responsible for it. We place expectations upon them that are not realistic. It's unfair – to them and to us.

Maybe you find yourself in this situation, drifting from one relationship to another expecting the next person to bring you that completeness. Maybe you are in a controlling relationship whereby you've let go of who you were before you entered that relationship. Your hobbies, goals and ambitions, those elements that define you as an individual, are cast aside, and the goals you previously desired are no longer significant. Before you realise it, you have lost so much of who you are for the sake of your relationship, to please the other individual, and in doing so, feed their insecurities as well. What proves a viable sacrifice is no longer significant.

We are continuously growing and evolving. When you get into a relationship, what you did prior to that may not necessarily work any longer, depending on whether it was a positive or negative behaviour. But if you had dreams or hobbies and you cannot bring them into your relationship, then you have to question is this the right person for you? But so many people lose themselves in their relationship, lose who they are, lose their voice, their ability to have fun, to have happiness and all for the sake of another and their demands, wants and desires.

Tony Gaskins said, "If you don't have a vision, then someone will hire you to build theirs'. We all have a vision of how we want our relationships to be or a vision for our future. So many people sacrifice their dreams because of relationships. Don't let that be you.

MONEY

Our dependency on money is one of the biggest causes of lack of sovereignty. We often sacrifice the dreams we had as children, of changing the world and becoming the next superhero. Many dreams we held on to as we grew up would still be possible if we had not been told to get real, get a job, pay the bills – as if that were enough. But the 'real world' has been designed, not for the average person to succeed and flourish, but the opposite, to keep them in a perpetual state of debt, fear and spending to feel good. They relinquish the driving force that has the ability to see them escape and reclaim their sovereignty and maintain it.

Self-governance is about taking responsibility to educate yourself. We use money day in, day out. It has shaped the world as we know it, yet many of us do not know how to use it. There are thousands of books available that will educate you on the best way to invest, the best way to save, how to make more out of your money, and all of the different strategies to take you potentially to financial independence, if that's what you're looking for. Yet hardly any of us take responsibility for this and educate ourselves.

FAMILY DYNAMICS

Lack of self-governance can also present itself in the family setting amongst your siblings or your parents. You may have lost your voice because you felt overpowered by those around you. Because it happened at such a young age, you've accepted it. Now you've adopted the backseat approach to life, letting others dictate how you should be and what you should do. We see it within parent and child relationships with the child always seeking approval from their parents. This overshadows their life and independence as they are bound to an emotional prison, in a never-ending cycle of seeking acceptance that they'll never receive. They live for the approval of their parents and allow them to dictate their future, the university they go to or the career they have. They allow their parents to determine their life without ever challenging them.

ILL HEALTH

When ill health hits you it can leave you feeling out of control, a victim without the power to shift that ailment. Helplessness creeps in. It's not the ailment itself but how it makes you feel helpless and out of control. A person who suffers from ill health may assume the patient role and lose their ability to make their own decisions. They are diagnosed by medical professionals and become reliant on doctors for medication. But doctors don't know everything. And much of what we hear isn't the truth because of the power of pharmaceutical companies, in whose interests it is that patients are prescribed drugs for their conditions rather than being educated on how to live a healthy lifestyle in the first place.

The Buck Stops with You

You must know that whatever you have in life starts and stops with you. Nature has equipped you with the mechanics to elevate you from the lower-level basement all the way to the private penthouse suite with rooftop views that most people only dream of. But dreams without action are for those who are sleeping. I am here to awaken you to your true power. No longer will you perceive any goal as being unattainable. When you self-govern, you take charge of any situation and redirect your life towards your chosen destination. You realise that the only thing that separates your current reality from your desired future is *you.*

YOU are in control of your destiny. You *are* the result of everything you've believed, thought and done. Where you are now is the result of everything you've done up to this point. You can no longer point the finger of blame at others: you are your own keeper. Until you accept this fact, you will not move forward to accept the life that awaits you. If we accept accountability for our own feelings, thoughts and actions, we can begin to self-govern.

I understand that there are many people experiencing unimaginable traumas, and my heart goes out to you. But I would say this: negative experiences need not define you or prevent you from reaching your potential. It is our true nature to be accountable for our own reality, good or bad.

What we get comes as a result of our expectations in life. We may have developed a belief that other people are responsible for making us happy and bringing us fulfilment, whether financially or in relationships – but we can't depend on others. We have to look within us. This responsibility lies with you – and you alone! Self-governance means that the buck stops with us. The answer to every question comes from within.

This realisation doesn't come easily – or we would all be living a life of happiness and there would be no need for me to write this book. And I too have been guilty of living in the slipstream of others, following other people's dreams and watching them prosper, without giving a thought to what it was that I wanted to achieve from life. Not valuing my own ability and presence in this world, I have waited for people to break me off a piece of the pie they held. But we have to make our own lives the priority.

Take Back Sovereignty

Take responsibility for your life and be proactive. Don't depend on anyone. You alone are responsible for making the changes needed to improve your life – not your boss, your family or your friends – just you! It may seem like an impossible task, but anyone who has turned their lives around for the better decided they were the only ones who could make that change.

Time and time again, people look for someone else to save them or hand them opportunities. They develop a dependency outside themselves, hoping another person will change their circumstances and give them happiness – which never comes.

To change your world, you have to *become the change*. You have to *be the difference*. Self-governance is not easy to achieve, which is why so few people apply it within their lives. But there are those who do – whether by reaching their boiling point or by deciding it was simply time for them to step into their own. They know it's their call, if they want things to change and they want something more from life.

Life has been devalued as a result of how we have been made to feel about ourselves. You cannot let your desire for self-governance override your true value. Freedom and life cannot be quantified or traded. Although not everyone is in a position to see life's real bounty, once you discover it, you immediately understand that nothing is worth sacrificing it for. If you knew your true majesty, you would not forfeit it.

Sometimes it is beneficial for us to release control to someone with more experience and knowledge who can help us. But there is a huge difference between receiving help and handing over our power. When we blindly accept all we are given by a 'higher authority' without questioning its truth, intent or origins, there's a problem!

Self-governance means taking control over all areas of your life – not being railroaded into making decisions that do not serve your higher self. We are repeatedly reminded what we can or cannot do – sometimes for our greater good, but the rest of the time this prevents us from reaching our true potential. Learn to remove the bullshit, to uncover a truth that will set you free to create happiness, joy and abundance.

Life is the greatest gift we'll ever be blessed to receive, but all too often our viewpoint prevents us from fully appreciating this. We must take charge of the life we have been gifted.

Shift Your Perspective

We get so bogged down by the meaningless detail of our daily existence; we may never see the bigger picture. In order to self-govern, you must shift your perspective and develop a wider outlook on life. Your relationship with yourself must also change. Often, a lack of progress is down to the poor relationship people have with themselves: lying to justify their lack of discipline or action, or exposing themselves to negative relationships or environments. Many people bury their heads in the sand and pretend that everything is okay, rather than facing reality. Self-governance is about looking within, discovering who you are, and understanding your motivations and which internal barriers prevent you from achieving what you want. Many people fear the opinions of others, allowing this to lead them away from their path. Self-governance is a form of self-love: accepting who you are, where you're at, and identifying who you need to be to move forward and grow.

BREAK THE CYCLE

This is all self-governance is: self-awareness – knowing who you are in this world, at any given time. Upon achieving self-awareness, you can determine if you want to remain in your present circumstances, and if not, you know that the power is within you to change them. Self-governance is the acceptance of responsibility for your life and everything within it. It is freedom, ownership and faith in all that is, and all that you can become.

If you know that there is an area in your life that you need to improve, don't shy away from taking action – even if it's just by finding out how you think and how to motivate yourself. Have the will and tenacity to decipher your internal mechanics and fine-tune your engine. This is one of the key attributes of those who successfully self-govern. Whatever your situation, if you want to take control of your life, you must start by working on yourself and forming an honest relationship with you.

HONESTY IS THE KEY

Whatever your predicament or reasoning, if you want to take control of your life, you must form an honest relationship with yourself. Start by scoring where you are now and where you want to be on a scale of 0 – 10, with 10 being exactly where you want to be in life. How far away from 10 are you now? Don't worry about your score too much. *The Success Rebellion* will help you to understand the ground you must cover to move closer to achieving a 10. There is no shame if you are worlds away from what you desire. You are already a step ahead just by examining it, as many people stay blinkered to it all their lives. You have to break the cycle and reflect upon where you are now, and doing so will gradually unearth what must be done to move you towards your goals.

LOOK AHEAD

The failings of the past no longer serve you, and where focus goes, energy flows. It's important for you to focus on who you want to be rather than the mistakes of your past. A new world awaits you with endless possibilities. Let go of any baggage that doesn't serve you, because the less you carry, the further you are likely to go.

DEDICATE SOME 'YOU TIME'

Who we truly are can often become lost within the noise of our busy lives. It's important you dedicate both space and time to re-establish your own personal connection with you. Remove any distractions, phones, TV, people and learn to spend time on your own. It is surprising how many people struggle with this, but when you are alone you will begin to notice your true feelings without being influenced. 'You Time' also allows you to rebuild the connection with your inner voice, which is the ultimate guidance system for success and happiness.

Become the Change

To move to a state of self-governance you need to make small incremental changes in your life on a weekly basis that over a period of time will create a huge shift. If you've been unwell, start to become more conscious of what you eat. If you rely on other people for your own happiness, take stock of where you're at and think about what changes you need to make improvements. Then make those small changes. That will create the momentum, like a snowball effect.

The chains that hold you will break, but this has to happen in order to free yourself and reach your goals. There may be risks in making change in your life. Things may break down at work or in your relationships. It will create friction with the people around you. They'll be fearful because you are changing and moving away from them; that's a natural part of growing and changing. Remember first and foremost that you have a responsibility to you, and you alone. In the same way as others are not responsible for your happiness, you are not responsible for theirs either. People will question what you're doing, even ridicule it, but it's necessary. So, be prepared for a rocky road, but I assure you, it's worth it.

This journey never ends. It's a voyage of continuous improvement, evolution, development and growth. You never really complete it. But the beauty of it is that the value isn't in the final destination. It's in the journey.

Summary

Somewhere along the line, with the pressures and realities of everyday life, we have lost our ability to govern ourselves, make our own decisions and live our own lives. Work, relationships, money, family and health all pull us away from fulfilling our own desires and prevent us from achieving the life we want. But we cannot just sit by and let this happen – we need to take back control.

Take responsibility for your own life, take back your sovereignty and take action. Reconnect with yourself, and what you want out of life. Shift your thinking, and become the change you want.

Reflection

Before you move on to the next chapter take a couple of minutes to think about these questions:

- Where have you lost sovereignty in your life?
- What will you start to change as a result of reading this chapter?

CHAPTER 2

Environment

What Is Environment?

Our adaptability to our environment is one of the key elements that has allowed human beings to flourish on this planet. Our ability to evolve according to our external influences has defined our success as human beings. However, this ability to merge with the outside world is also responsible for our downfall, for there are many environments that are not conducive to who we are as humans, and so we adjust our behaviours in order for us to survive these sometimes toxic surroundings. This adaptability also explains why we can lose sovereignty when we adapt to circumstances outside of our control.

Your environment and all of its different elements have shaped your very being and made you the person that you are today.

Your external stimuli, the things you are exposed to, influence you in ways that you can't even imagine. Your home life, family dynamics, friendships, school, music, TV, what you read, what you eat, what you see, in fact anything you are able to sense, will have an effect on who you are. (There is also what we can't perceive, but that is a book in itself.)

Key Aspects of Environment

Your physical environment, including where you live, where you work and where you chose to spend your time, has a direct impact on who you are. It can imprison you and prevent you from seeing or experiencing what life truly has to offer. Or it can elevate you, nurturing your being and providing you with the self-belief, network and resources necessary to create the life you want. It is important to regulate your environment to ensure that it reflects who you want to become. I was totally unaware of what I was truly capable of until I stepped out of the environment that I had grown up in. It was only when I experienced a new environment, which provided me with a new perspective, that I realised how much my surroundings and the people around me had held me back. If I had not had the opportunity to experience this new perspective, then it is likely that I would have further succumbed to my environment and set my expectations accordingly. By stepping out of my environment I was able to form a new point of reference and realise exactly what was possible. I'm not saying that I had the know-how to attain these new found possibilities, but I didn't need to. What was important was that, in my mind, a new landscape had been formed and a new sense of possibilities achieved.

If your environment makes you who you are, then it follows that you need to think about what you can do to change it, if you are not living the life you want. There are two aspects to this: 1) how your being is affected by what is around you, and 2) the role your family and friends play in whether you achieve your goals or not.

How Your Environment Influences Your Being

I interviewed Dr. Richard Bandler, cocreator of NLP (Neuro-Linguistic Programming), who said:

> You must understand that you're being indoctrinated with

> beliefs all the time. No matter where you come from, people around you are always building beliefs. You can either look at yourself as the rule, or you look at yourself as the exception. If most of the people in a neighbourhood believe they are going to stay in that neighbourhood and economic class, you too can either continue to believe that or build a new belief that goes on the exception, 'I'm getting out of here, I'm going up and I'm going to do something with my life.' And if you do that your time has to stretch out, so that how you spend the moments in the next 60 seconds, the next 60 days, the next 6 years all becomes important! So that the years after all become years where you are successful and your only question is how to become even more successful.

What often takes place within a particular area or social group is a level of collective thought, meaning and a shared way of thinking. Many people who live in lower-income or disadvantaged areas share similar thoughts of scarcity and lack when it comes to financial matters. Such repeated thoughts tend to form beliefs around unworthiness and can lead to language such as 'good things never happen to me' or 'it's not for people like us'. An 'Us and Them' culture grows as they identify themselves separately from the abundance that is being received elsewhere. These disempowering beliefs become deep rooted and influence the behaviours and actions of those who live in the area.

Disadvantaged areas are prone to high rates of crime, and this has a direct impact on those people who live or work there. And so they are, often unconsciously, locked into a state of fear and stress which directly affects how they interact on a daily basis within these surrounding environments.

Immersing yourself in a new environment, an environment that reflects your goals and ambitions, is a crucial part of success. If you know that your current environment is holding you back, then it's your responsibility to identify the environment that will push you forward and complement your dreams. Set goals accordingly, and make it a habit to put yourself in places that reflect the future life you want to achieve.

Friends and Family Influences

Equally, who you spend time with, which can be described as your social environment, also influences your being. It is said that you become the average of the people that you spend the most time with, as the people in your immediate sphere of influence will have an effect on you. This can be the difference between success and failure. It's essential that you understand this principle and realise just how much influence your immediate network has on your current reality. Sometimes we unconsciously take on some of their mannerisms or language. Words that were not previously within our vocabulary start to pop up in our daily chitchat. The longer we spend with certain people, the more influence they have, and this can either have a positive or negative effect on you and your journey!

The relationships you form can literally make or break you. Within a family dynamic there may be underlying issues that cause emotional blockages that prevent you from moving towards your goals. Such as when parents have too much control over a child's life, imposing an oppressive regime and dictating how they should live, rather than allowing a child to live their life according to their desires. Or it may be sibling rivalry, competition with your brother or sister that has played out since childhood and still has a negative impact on you, bringing up emotions of not being good enough and never allowing you to truly feel your sense of power. I am not suggesting you sever your family ties but that becoming mindful of your family dynamics provides you with greater control on how best to reduce the impact of an inharmonious family dynamic.

Friends could be regarded as the family we have chosen, and so obviously we have to choose wisely. What are the topics of conversation amongst those around you? Do you have friends that are energy suckers and adopt an 'all about me' approach and just take, take, take? Do your friends encourage you to become better, or do they resent you even trying? In order to rise above your current circumstances, you have to look seriously at those around you and vet anyone you allow into your immediate sphere of influence.

Your friends and your bonds should lift you higher. Our relationships are hard to compare, as they differ from person-to-person and different friendships bring different things. But you must begin to identify how they make you feel and whether they truly complement where you want to be in life. If you realise that some of your friendships are not encouraging you in your life plans or helping your mindset, then set your intent to form new connections with those who want similar things in life. This needs to be an equal exchange, as your friendship should offer as much to them as theirs does to you.

Those who are born into the upper echelons or society, whether here in the UK or abroad, are taught the power of their network from an early age. Choices around schooling and university aren't solely made on the quality of their grades or the reputation of a particular professor but are largely based upon the connections that will be formed while attending these institutions. Schools such as Eton, Cambridge or Harvard are chosen because their parents know the importance of establishing friendships within the right circles and how this will dramatically increase their chances of success in the future when they venture out into the wider world.

Likewise, high-flying professionals and business people across the world also understand the correlation between social networks and financial success. These individuals pay high membership fees to belong to exclusive members clubs where they rub shoulders with the most successful people in business, finance and entertainment. These clubs provide them with a network that enhances their progress and ambitions. Many join multiple clubs to secure direct access to people who can add value to their journey. They know the importance of establishing friendships within the right circles and how this dramatically increases their chances of achieving success in life.

Having an awareness of how these two aspects of your environment impact your life is key to you realising your goals. If you choose to remain anchored to an environment that stifles your chances of success or surround yourself with people who have a negative influence on you, you will not create the life you want to lead. Take action on this today. Decide on what you need to do to change your environment so that you can begin to move steadily towards your goal of a better future.

Never Let Your Environment Dictate Who You Are!

I don't remember having any real role models when growing up. The people in my life were neither good nor bad. I have two older brothers as well as older cousins who could be deemed as negative role models if I had had a closer relationship with them. But mostly during my younger years I was fairly innocent and oblivious to the world around me. However, as I entered my late teens I slowly succumbed to the reality of my environment, and my behaviour also changed to match it. What is important here is that you don't often realise you have been brought up in a negative environment because it is your norm. It is the only reality that you've experienced, and so you have nothing to compare it to. It is only when you form a new point of reference and step out from that environment that has held you back that you start to understand. By moving out of East London, forming new relationships and broadening my horizons, meeting new people and engaging in new activities, I slowly started to step out of my old life and began to see it for what it was.

The Ever-Lasting Impression of Your Role Models

It's widely agreed that there is a lack of positive role models in today's society. We know that being brought up in a secure environment with positive influences is likely to increase your chances of becoming a more rounded, happy and successful individual. However, the opposite is also true. Bad parenting, negative conditions and poor behavioural influences lead you towards bad decisions and life choices that prevent you harnessing your true ability. Yet even with this knowledge and understanding of the value of good role models, we are subjected to a daily bombardment across every medium – entertainment, film, music and celebrity – of people; positioned as role models, yet they do not show the values or moral principles that we would wish our sons or daughters to learn. In past times, the role models in our communities would have been the village elders or people within stories, myths or legends, with their values and teachings passed down from generation to generation. But now we see a movement towards characters that reflect the darker aspects of human nature. And strangely, we feel comfortable in this new norm. So what's changed?

Today's role models no longer display the values of their predecessors but instead adopt an almost sinister demeanour, be they characters in films, programmes or cartoons. They often promote traits of violence, retribution and ego. The advancement of technology has exposed us to a new system of entertainment, forcing the darker aspects of human nature upon our daily experience, and so sadly a generation has naively subscribed to these idols, allowing the influences to shape our being. Could it be that a bigger agenda is at hand, one that fully understands the inner mechanics of the human psyche and its susceptibility to manipulation through the subconscious mind?

So much of what we now believe has been communicated through the medium of TV or news. We think that if it's on TV, it must be true. What is scary is how these narratives shape us. We live in a time when many people believe what they are told. For instance, that Islam means terrorism. The other myths we are sold are that beauty is only achieved through cosmetics, and that we have to be rich to be happy.

Let's take each of these myths in turn. The truth is that Islam is a beautiful and peaceful religion with much of its teachings and rituals misunderstood by the Western world. The very essence of the word *Islam* derives from the root word *Sal'm* which means peace. As for beauty, true beauty only radiates from within! Physical attraction may catch your attention, but only inner beauty can ever hold it.

And finally, although wealth seems like the answer to your problems, money alone will never make you happy, whereas being happy will always make you rich!

Don't let TV or social media be your role model by shaping what you believe.

The importance of the mentor or role model has been incredibly underestimated.

It goes far beyond the offerings of friendly advice, career guidance or life coaching. When you choose your mentors, consciously or unconsciously, you are committing to a direct transference of knowledge, experience and behaviour that may either hinder or empower you depending on who your mentor is.

I believe you take on the characteristics of those who you identify with, meaning you don't have to be in that person's presence in order to form a connection. This can be done remotely or just by pure intent. By studying someone's life or teachings, you form energetic connections. You embrace their ethos and connect with their life force. As you learn more and study their path, you are drawn to emulate that with which you resonate. The closer their journey is to yours, the more similarities they share and the more you will connect with them.

In order for you to succeed and truly win in your own Success Rebellion, it is best practice to adopt behaviours from individuals who live their life according to a higher set of values and demonstrate a positive way of living.

When you choose a mentor, you agree to take on parts of their programming.

If you make your decision consciously, then your goal is to embrace their positive traits and the characteristics that drew you to them. Your decision should be based upon wanting to grow. Therefore, seek the navigational tools that will help you to achieve your goal, whatever that may be.

It is therefore essential to form the correct relationships with the right mentors or role models, finding ones that serve your cause. Even though you may be drawn to someone's achievements or particular aspects of their career, be aware that the darker side of that mentor may outweigh the more positive characteristics. The mentee becomes inspired by the achievements of their mentor and unconsciously emulates the behaviours that directly led to them achieving their success. And so a similar life pattern will begin to appear in your life. When good mentoring relationships are formed, the rate of success for the mentee can be out of this world.

We see evidence of this in many of the global names and brands that are well known today. Without the correct mentorship or role model, it's unlikely they would have achieved these heights of success. When you unravel the journey of elite performers, the ultra-rich and the success stories, you will discover that through most of their journey, there was someone who acted in the capacity of a mentor or role model for them. Whether it was someone they looked up to or to someone who guided them along the way, there was that special someone who they turned to for advice or guidance and whose behaviours, habits and attitude they emulated.

Yves Saint Laurent was just eighteen when Christian Dior gave him his start. He quickly gained Dior's trust and so became his pupil, learning much of Dior's wisdom, secrets and fashion expertise. Steve Jobs of Apple famously mentored Mark Zuckerberg after Zuckerberg reached out to him in the early days of starting Facebook.

Cristiano Ronaldo, who is undeniably one of the greatest footballers of all time, would not be where he is today if it wasn't for the mentorship of Sir Alex Ferguson, who was his manager during his time at Manchester United. Despite his natural talent, Ronaldo lacked many attributes that were necessary to make his true mark on football. Under Ferguson's guidance, Ronaldo slowly grew into the player he is today. Without Ferguson's influence it is likely Ronaldo would have remained a mediocre player with a bag of tricks but little real impact within a game.

You see, in order for you to grow, you must be willing to learn and accept the wisdom of others. People who are where you want to be and who hold the expertise and the insight to guide you there. Their guidance is important to your success, so choose your role model wisely.

Just to recap:

1. Identify someone who is where you want to be in life. Someone who you can relate to and has travelled a similar path to you and who displays the strength, skills and attributes that you wish to emulate. Follow their journey. Do they blog, post content on social channels, or have they published a book? Success leaves trails, so it's for you to track their journey.
2. Make the approach only after you've done your research. And don't let your enthusiasm get the better of you; refrain from putting forward your proposition too soon.
3. Reach out to the prospective mentor requesting an informal chat over coffee or lunch.

Although I never had the benefit of a one on one mentor relationship at the start of my journey, this didn't stop my success, as I found my mentors in books to help me in the journey. Reading gave me access to the teachings of many different experts and gurus on the subjects of entrepreneurism, wealth, success, spirituality and transformation. As well as reading, I made the commitment to attend workshops and short courses, and was able to establish my own philosophy according to what worked best for me.

Our Working Environment

Not enough thought is given to how much our working environment impacts our health and wellbeing. Most of us spend the majority of our waking lives at work, and yet we fail to see just how our working environment affects our physical and emotional health. Cities have become unnatural habitats, man-made concrete jungles, with little to no access to trees or greenery. Stuck in the confines of our offices, many of us are surrounded by computers and other electromagnetic devices spewing their toxic waves across all within their vicinity. Many employees work without much sunlight, and some hardly see daylight, causing deficiencies in Vitamin D and low levels of serotonin. It is reported by Harvard School of Public Health that over one billion people worldwide are suffering from Vitamin D deficiency, and a large contributor to this is the lack of sunlight due to a decreasing amount of time spent outdoors.

We also work in stressful environments, often jumping from one task to another, with adrenal glands pumping overtime in a continuous state of fight or flight. In the city, everything operates at a million miles an hour, unlike in the countryside where you'll find that life is more in tune with the correct pace of life and falls into a natural rhythm. City environments can be productive for corporations who need to centralise their operations, but they can be very toxic for the health and wellbeing and personal happiness of the people who work within them.

The success of coffee franchises over the past decade is testament to how we have become dependent on the consumption of coffee in order to function at the demand that has been set. When the Spanish colonised parts of South America they encouraged the use of the coca plant to increase productivity amongst its enslaved indigenous workforce. The coffee bean now serves a similar purpose within global business culture, with our city streets lined with outlets that keep the workforce churning at maximum capacity.

You have to become aware and educate yourself on just how the environments you spend time in have an effect on your vitality and overall welfare.

Summary

Your environment shapes who you are. Everything you are exposed to – family, work colleagues, TV and social media – affects who and what you will become.

It is essential to surround yourself with positive energy wherever you live and particularly where you work. Be aware of picking up the negative energy of your colleagues, of the impact of your social life, and how your lifestyle affects your health and mindset.

Role models are essential to your success. Choose someone who has been on the same pathway as you. Research them well, and then emulate their achievements.

Reflection

Take time to think about the following questions:

- Is your environment geared towards helping you with your future hopes and dreams?
- If not, what must you do in order to change your environment for the better?
- What sort of environment DOES complement your future goals?
- What connections do you need to form in order for you to level up?
- Who do you know who is already where you want to be?
- Who inspires you through their achievements and success?
- What behaviours do they display? What are their strengths?
- What do they read or talk about?

CHAPTER 3

Discovering Your Path

We've looked at the importance of self-governance and shaping your environment to serve you, and choosing the right mentor for your Success Rebellion journey. Now let's look at how to discover your path in life.

It is said that we are always one choice away from a completely different life and that each action triggers a reaction and sends a ripple effect across the entire universe. No matter how big or small, your choices set in motion the events and synchronicity that influence and impact your present moment as well as that of your future. Your choices are so powerful that they have consequences for the wider world around you and everything within it, which can impact the lives of millions daily without you ever knowing.

Understanding how the choices you make directly impact your life is of great importance for success and growth. If your past choices have repeatedly pulled you down the rabbit hole, then it is time to make new choices because continuing to do what you have always done will only create more of what you have already had. You must create a new reality by making choices that are attuned to the future reality you wish to create.

However, don't place too much pressure and judgment upon yourself every time you make a decision which doesn't go to plan. No one is perfect, and there will be times when the wrong decisions are made! The road to success is lined with mistakes, failures and 'bad decisions' that are a necessary component of the learning process. Without these experiences we would never achieve the learning outcomes that shape us into who we need to be to achieve our vision. There is no such thing as a bad decision, as the essence of life is about experience, both the good and the bad. I deem both opposites as necessary in order for you to learn, grow and evolve as a human being. But this does not give you permission to live a life repeating the same old patterns and making the same mistakes time and time again. The point I am making is not about playing it safe and avoiding mistakes, but about ensuring the daily choices you make, whether big or small, steer you towards a better quality of life. Sometimes, to disrupt your old patterns, you need to break some rules to help take you in a new direction that elevates you higher and brings harmony into your everyday existence.

This brings me to emotional awareness. One of the key drivers influencing your decision-making is in fact, your emotions. They possess the power to either guide you towards greatness, or to be the catalyst for destruction.

Most of the world's elite performers and highly successful people understand the power of strengthening their emotional awareness, and they actively work on doing so. Developing a strong emotional awareness is crucial to overcoming the impulsive behaviours that may lead you away from your true path. The emotions you feel drive your behaviour. Learning to manage these emotions will put you in the driving seat of your life.

Stored unconscious emotions from past experiences can prevent us from stepping into that driving seat. Negative past experiences can haunt us for years. The emotions stay imprinted and play out when the subconscious mind detects a similar threat. To develop a strong emotional intelligence is to become aware of these emotions and acknowledge them, without surrendering and allowing them to drive your behaviour. Only then will you establish the clear perspective that will help you with your own Success Rebellion. This also relates to other people and recognising the emotions within them and how they can affect both their and your behaviour. This will enable you to hack into your biochemistry and override your emotional programming, so that better decisions and choices can be made.

I'm not saying you should develop narcissistic traits and block your emotions altogether, but the decisions made whilst experiencing high states of negative emotion don't tend to be our best. How many times have you said something to your partner in the heat of an argument only to regret it hours later? Emotions can cause us to behave and act in ways that are totally unrecognisable and out of character.

Many of the people who are currently in prison are there as a result of a bad choice made within a highly emotional time. If they had the tools to see through the emotion, it is likely that the outcome would have been far different. No matter what your situation, developing an emotional awareness is an essential skill in order to make better choices in life that will take you forward to where you want to be.

Accepting Your Past

Once you become mindful of your emotions, you no longer allow them to dictate your future. You release yourself from the bondage of past traumas instead of allowing them to be a source of disempowerment. By accepting your past and facing your shadows, you uncover the treasures and gifts that lie hidden within them. It's easy to view the past solely as a time of regret and negativity because of mistakes you've made, the traumas you've experienced and bridges you've burnt. Embracing your past is vital for your future success. MY POINT ISN'T to REJECT YOUR PAST BUT to LEARN FROM IT so that IT WILL HAVE BEEN VALUABLE TO YOU. Your history and journey is what makes you you!

Often, your life's mission, your purpose and your gifts come about as a byproduct of your past. Your journey provides you with the conditioning, training and experience to step into your life's work. Up to now you may have gone through life labelling every experience either good or bad in order to make some sense of the world. You have to let go of your judgments and understand that experiencing contrast is necessary to learn. Therefore, embrace your history and your story, because your purpose is an integral part of that journey.

Nelson Mandela would never have been able to achieve what he did had he not been imprisoned. That was a necessary part of his life in order for him to go on to capture the attention and win the hearts and the minds of not just the people of South Africa but also the world. Had he not been oppressed because of the colour of his skin and then released decades after – shaking hands as an expression of forgiveness with the very same people who were responsible for his imprisonment in the first place – then it's unlikely he would have become president of South Africa and a global icon.

Tony Robbins talks openly about the abuse he experienced as a child from his mother. Because of that, he felt an undying desire to ensure that other people didn't have to go through the same experience. That spurred him on to become the person he needed to be to help others, so that they didn't have to continue living with the experience of their past traumas and emotional heartache. Had he not grown up in those conditions, he would not have been driven to become the world's leading self-help guru and life coach, with an estimated value of $500 million dollars. What we sometimes deem as being negative and shy away from in our past is often the key to the future and an opportunity to discover our life's purpose.

The Importance of Your Story

What I'm talking about here is a reframing of your story. From feeling like a victim of your life and circumstances to visualize being the hero of your own story, where you journey on your own Success Rebellion. No amount of blaming others, self pity and feeling sorry for yourself will never change your circumstances – a harsh but true fact! People aren't going to rush to your aid and be compelled to help you simply because life has been difficult; this isn't how it works! There are millions of people out there, all with a story much worse and much more challenging than yours, so to even try and compete makes no sense at all. So do you continue to allow your circumstances to not only define your past but to also determine your future, or do you begin to reframe your story and change the narrative within it, moving from a position of victim to someone of empowerment and purpose, giving your life a whole different meaning? Use your past as a means to leverage your future; consider it to be your competitive advantage, and so you must learn to seek the opportunity within it.

Pain is sometimes the source of our greatest work. Had Shah Jahan not experienced the death of his beloved wife whilst giving birth to their fourteenth child, it is likely that he would never have been inspired to commission one of the greatest wonders the world has ever seen, the Taj Mahal.

As hard as it may be, we have to accept who we are and that everything up until now was necessary to bring us this point. You have the ability to develop a new chapter, taking into account the teachings of the past and using your experience to define a new purpose for you and your life.

For me, my Success Rebellion story is about the transformation I have made. I started at the very bottom with little money or opportunities. My aspirations were minimal with ambitions to match, and so, like many people in that situation, I first thought that the only way I could access the level of success I wanted was by taking the lower road.

When I looked honestly at the dead end that life would have taken me to, with inevitable outcomes, it was clear that I had to carve out a different path for myself. A path that would require me to step up and lead me to embrace a higher set of values and a new perspective of what was truly possible.

I've learned a lot from my journey from a place without privilege, and so I feel able and qualified to help others who are at similar crossroads, of being asleep to the opportunities around them, unaware of how they can rewrite their future story and begin their own Success Rebellion.

I am living proof that a successful and fulfilling life transformation can be achieved, and I know my purpose is to help make that same change happen for others.

Natural Ability

When we enter this life we bring and develop a special set of gifts that are exclusive to us. Perhaps you are an excellent public speaker. Or you're a natural comedian and always the centre of attention and laughter amongst friends or family. Maybe you are a great athlete with a competitive mindset that pushes you beyond others, so that you are the best in any activity you pursue. These are all examples of skills that we naturally possess and were given to share with the world in order to enhance both our and the lives of others.

The problem is that through schooling or family circumstances, we often compromise our gifts and natural abilities in order to fit in and meet the expectations of society or those around us. Schools fail miserably in recognising pupils' unique abilities, as they are generally not structured to develop pupils on an individual basis. The curriculum teaches outdated concepts, delivered within an outdated model. Schools do not encourage individualism and are built upon the principle of educating all students to a set standard across the board, not honouring the individual key strengths of any one pupil. The majority of us pass through the education system not ever identifying what we naturally excel at, or if we do, no huge value is placed upon it, and the opportunity of their skill set is never fully explored. Students are then readied to become employees, further entrenching them into a life that does not harness their true potential but instead provides wages as a substitute for happiness.

To escape this trap you have to remember who you are. What do you enjoy? What comes easy to you? What did you dream of being when growing up? What stirs your passion? You have to join the dots together in order to see the bigger picture at hand.

YOU not being everything that YOU are and can be builds invisible barriers that prevent YOU from achieving your highest potential. We were not born to be standardised or to become carbon copies of everyone else. Your power lies within your uniqueness, and so YOU must begin to uncover what makes YOU different and what makes YOU special.

I see many people with big dreams who do not use the one thing that could catapult them to where they want to be. They do not recognise or place value upon the gift they have and never get to experience the opportunities that it offers.

Happiness, success and freedom can be found by embracing who you are and using your natural gifts to map a new future. This is a challenge in itself. Letting go of everything you have previously been taught is no easy task. But condemning yourself to a continuous life of nothingness and pretending everything is okay is not easy either. Our biggest achievements are hidden behind our biggest fears, so you have to make the choice of happiness and allow this to be your guiding light.

I interviewed Patrick Wanis, PhD, celebrity life coach & human behaviour expert, on this issue and he said:

> If you want to properly prepare people for life then you must give them proper tools for life. Those tools cannot be limited to physics, mathematics or problem solving; the proper tools must involve and develop self-awareness. If you go back to the age of Socrates and Plato, you find that psychology comes from philosophy; that's the origin of psychology (the study of human thought and behaviour). And the philosophy of Socrates, Plato, Aristotle and others is the focus on the good life.
>
> Are we teaching people today in schools the ways to live a good life?
>
> The good life isn't a reference to drugs, sex, material possessions or simply freedom of expression; the good life refers to health, harmony, reasoning, knowledge, inquiry, music, artistic creation, love, and above all, meaning and purpose in life.
>
> Can you release yourself from emotional pain and trauma of past experiences? Can you change your subconscious beliefs?
>
> Can you engage emotional intelligence and make a positive difference in the world in alignment with your values and

passion? Can you learn how to not base your inner happiness on everything that's external? These are the things that are not being taught in school.

Wanis reaffirms why so many of us are experiencing a level of displacement within our lives. We are given the tools and some instruction on how to navigate aspects of the external world, but no guidance is ever given on the exploration of our inner worlds. The gifts, skills and creativity that lie within, waiting to be expressed through us. This is the path towards living a good life, by becoming self-aware and finding who we truly are!

The Greatest Enemy of Man

Once you connect the dots you realise that this newfound world of opportunity requires sacrifice to become who you are. This is the biggest challenge for all, letting go of the idea of who you thought you were and overcoming the fear that imprisons you within this false reality. Fear is the biggest cause of inaction, procrastination and suffering. This emotion is disabling but is prevalent in most people.

The biggest fear that prevents us from taking our true path is the fear of how others may judge us. We form an avatar or character as a means of protection, and we play out this role and associate ourselves as this construct we have created. But this is not who you are! It's the identity you've formed to survive in this world.

The essence of who you are is love, and your gifts were given as a form of love. To tap into their potential and reconnect with your gifts, you first have to get back to a place of love. This takes great courage and strength, as those who are not of that nature will fail to understand your logic. Don't let their ignorance prevent you stepping into your majesty.

As a snake must shed its skin or a caterpillar becomes a butterfly, you have to let go of the old self in order to transform into something else. Your actions may not always gain the support and encouragement from those around you, and very often it's their judgement that prevents us being who we are destined to be. You have to break through that barrier of fear, undeterred by how you may be perceived by the outside world.

My biggest breakthroughs in life have always come once I had shifted my behaviours away from the false and fixed persona I had created for myself. As I moved towards alignment with my true self, it required a metamorphosis away from old habits and ways of being that those around me have not always understood. The question was: Should I stop my progress in the hope that other people might come round to my way of thinking, or do I embrace who I am and be confident that I am being authentically me? In order to truly experience happiness, you have to be authentic to who you are, and you have to let go of former conditioning and beliefs. You have to remove disguises you've worn and step into your brilliance.

Default Thinking

One of the biggest changes you have to make to discover your path is the shift from our default of 'I' to the place of 'we'. This is very different to how we are conditioned to operate, because our society is predominantly built upon the 'how this benefits me' culture. In an election, most people vote according to their own needs and how it will affect their lives rather than thinking about the community or nation as a whole. Business owners are generally inclined to vote conservative because the legislation is likely to favour them when it comes to business and personal taxes. Likewise, if you are on the lower end of the financial spectrum you might opt for parties that adopt more socialistic principles to bring more equality into society by perhaps raising income taxes for higher earners. Either way, all parties will attempt to influence your vote by promising YOU a better world according to YOUR wants if you pledge your support. Politicians or parties will never try to sway your thinking by sharing how their manifesto will benefit your neighbour, work colleague or the man who lives on the other side of town. They know how our minds work and generally it's fixed on the 'I' and very rarely on the 'we'.

The key to success is to move to from a focus on what you receive to a place of giving and serving others. In this way, you will get an understanding of the lack of meaning that a pre-Success Rebellion life has. The quick endorphin rush from a shopping spree lasts only a few minutes, whereas the feeling of reward when truly gifting someone from the heart is timeless. Being of service isn't about doing a 5k sponsored run with your work colleagues just to say that you give back and having the Instagram posts to prove it. It's about being present with the positive intent of uplifting someone else's life for the better and making that a part of your daily process and who you are. To understand true success, your path and vision for the future must in some way encompass the elevation of others, enhancing other lives so that yours too can be genuinely enriched with a currency that money could never buy. Your true path is for the betterment of yourself and perhaps for humanity too, for if it weren't, then why would you be reading this book? Think of this as a directional post pointing you towards where you should be heading, true north! By using your given talents in this way, you will complete your mission, giving total alignment with who you are and all that you are to become.

Once you do this, you move into the natural flow of creation. You will see an uplifting in more areas of your life. And once you align with this, you become aware of the synchronicities, the magic of life, the communication of this universal energy, and how it communicates to you on a daily basis, through events or coincidences which you then must listen to. Life becomes effortless because things fall into place naturally. That is when you achieve the greatest success. It's about letting go of control and allowing life to move through you, and being open to the opportunities that present to you. That is about following life's call. Listen to it. Follow it and see where it takes you. Don't let fear hold you back and make you think you can't do it. Even when you perceive things as not going to plan, this is a necessary part of your journey in order for you to step up. These challenges give us the experience and the learning that enables us to move forward and be who we need to be in order to achieve our goals.

Embrace your authentic self. Own it and allow the opportunities to take you forward.

Summary

Your story is your 'golden ticket' that will give you a competitive advantage in whatever field you want to enter into. It will give you a competitive advantage in life. Look at your past experiences, and identify the ones that can help you create your successful future.

Face any and all of your fears or you will stay where you are most comfortable and never seek out the opportunities the universe has created for you.

Change your default thinking from 'I' to 'we'. Only then will you change your life and the lives of others around you.

Listen to what the universe is saying to you. This is your life's message. Then take the steps to become the person you want to be.

Reflection

- What do you naturally excel at?
- What activities did you gravitate to as a child?
- What were your strengths at school?
- What old behaviours no longer serve your future self?

CHAPTER 4

What Is Vision?

With an appreciation for how your environment has impacted your life, an understanding that you must take back your power, and a strong sense of finding your path, we will move on to look at shaping your vision.

True vision goes far beyond your normal line of sight. It isn't what you can see in the here and now but an idea of a future that sits outside of your current reality. Essentially, it's your long-term goal, It's a glimpse of a future possibility that is not bound by your current circumstances, restrictions, and limitations. Consider it to be your ideal destination along your given journey, and by defining your vision of the future, you begin to establish a new point of reference to head towards. You begin to develop a natural sense of direction – an underlying mission that you are compelled to complete. Once you establish a higher vision, it naturally begins to invoke a magnetic force that pulls you towards it. No matter what challenges or obstacles are put before you, once you have invoked a strong vision, you will rise to each and every challenge, shaping your being to whom you must become in order to achieve your end goal.

The vision you have may be a million miles from where you are today. But once it has been set and you commit to taking action, you move steadily and surely towards where you choose to be. From there, you begin your journey of change and transformation. Those that have achieved massive success and shaped the world in some way have all shared that underlying driving force. They've all had a great sense of purpose, a greater underlying meaning to their existence and why they do what they do.

Having a vision gives life meaning, which in turn sparks a deeper desire to achieve your end goal. A vision for the future can and will totally change your perspective and outlook on life. It will give guidance on where you should focus your energies. And having this purpose will automatically raise the vibrancy of life. Tasks and duties that were once perceived as mundane can be given new life or meaning and approached with a new sense of excitement.

To be without a vision results in what I call 'average-ism'. You feel as though you are not making progress, as though you aren't growing as an individual, and you can experience high levels of dissatisfaction. Without a strong vision you may fall under the spell of someone else's vision, whether that be an individual, a group or societal norms. Your lack of imagination will bind you to serve the needs of another, who understands the power that this principle holds. In failing to create your own vision, like in a game of chess, you become the pawn and at any given time can be sacrificed in order for the real players to secure their win.

Unfortunately, this is the reality for so many, but it does not have to be yours. You do not have to accept any less than you deserve and anything other than the expectation that you set for yourself. Your vision is, in essence, your expectation, and without it you get swept along accepting life as it is, no longer dreaming of what you may become. Your conditioning is such that your thoughts are no longer your own, and like the majority of people, it's the fear that you hold that prevents you from ever truly making a stand.

Your vision is the missing link to fill the void that comes into your experience, that emptiness and niggling feeling of 'is this it?'. What I'm sharing with you is the gateway to a world of new possibilities. Instead of retracing your steps over and over again in a circle of despair, you can break the cycle and begin to form a clear destination to which you now must move towards. For the first time in a long time you will have clarity and will no longer have a dependency upon others and forces that sit outside of you. For your vision brings balance and alignment with nature's plan. We are here to grow, learn and experience to our highest potential. We are to live on the edge of possibility, challenging ourselves at any given opportunity. Rather than blindly stumbling along, or floating through life with no direction, allowing the wind to dictate your journey, create a vision that you take control of and harness the wind to your benefit, so that it propels you where you choose to go.

We have a choice in how we live. But we are so influenced by society that very few of us think beyond our current reality. You don't have to work in a nine-to-five job like everybody else. You have a choice! You don't have to live merely for the weekend. You have a choice! Your life doesn't have to revolve around the area you were born or raised. You have a choice! You can be as creative and imaginative as you want to be. You can be whoever or whatever you want; this is the power of the vision, and it is yours to do as you choose! SO WHAT WILL YOU CHOOSE? HOW WILL YOU KNOW WHAT TO CHOOSE?

Artistry

Put aside any negative forces that have shaped you to this point in your life, and think of your future as a blank canvas, upon which you can paint whatever you choose. If you had a magic wand and there was nothing holding you back, what would your life goals be? What do you want in life? We all have a rich creativity within us, waiting to be used. If your belief system or your thoughts limit you – adjust them. We are not limited beings. You might already be happy, and if so, that's fantastic. But imagine the possibilities and how much better your life could be, with the right additions or alterations to your mindset and to the way you live.

Every civilisation, ancient and modern, was built upon a vision. Likewise, some of the most influential companies of this era have achieved success through the power of their founders' overriding objectives – Steve Jobs and Apple, Mark Zuckerberg and Facebook, Richard Branson and Virgin to name a few. The more creative, dynamic and imaginative the vision, the wider the boundaries of normality expand, producing magic that will transform the landscape of the planet.

Some people have a vision entirely focused on material gain. Because this feeds into the ego, focusing solely on acquiring material possessions, it risks jeopardising your values and integrity. However, when you attach your journey to a higher purpose – beyond yourself and your own perceived need or 'greed' – you avoid the temptation of taking the low road to satisfy your own needs. What greater good can you do in the world? Wealth and material possessions often come as a byproduct of that greater purpose. But they should not be the sole purpose.

Clarity is key to the visualisation process. You need to know exactly where you want to be in order to get there. Without a clear destination to head towards, you risk travelling aimlessly or being blown off course. Be clear and precise in identifying what you want. Don't leave anything to chance. Be absolutely certain what you want to achieve. Make it crystal clear and concrete. Write it down and make a plan. Clarity is certainty, and it eliminates any doubt that could hinder your path to success.

Reliving Old Programmes

A Success Rebellion needs an objective for the future, or we get stuck, as we tend to live our lives based on past experiences, which stumps our personal growth. If we were to step back and take a look at our lives, we would see that the majority of the decisions we make are based upon these experiences and the impact they have made on us. But having a vision requires you to execute new behaviour in order for you to change your circumstances. Where you are right now is a result of everything you knew previously; therefore, in order to make change, you have to have a new perspective, a new direction.

Take a look around you. Do you see people who live just for the weekend? As soon as Monday comes, they can't wait for Friday. That makes five days in the week they are writing off. It's sad to think some people are unhappy five days out of seven. They miss the excitement and the learning and the enjoyment of being in the present, and neglect the here and now because they are so focused on reaching the end of the week.

You can dream of a better life, and you may have an idea of where you want to be, but unless you put in a specific destination into your sat nav, you could end up absolutely anywhere.

So start now to define the elements of what your dream life really looks like or you will never achieve it. If you can't visualise your future life in detail, you can't reach that destination.

Why Do We Lack Vision?

As we discussed in Self-Governance, the system that we have inherited does not help us to envisage a better future for ourselves. Modern life and its distractions have conditioned us to become narrow minded rather than free thinking. Our education systems, that are supposed to equip us with the knowledge, skills and tools to prosper, fail us on many levels and in fact encourage us to conform to a reality that does not provide us with any real benefits. Our education institutions do not encourage creativity or engagement with the imaginative mind. As a consequence, we become linear in thought and are pulled away from the gifts that we hold, which are necessary for us to step into our brilliance. We accept the beliefs and the general consensus of society, failing to question the integrity of the institutions that have influence on the population. We are conditioned to accept a system whereby we are sold the dream that if you work hard enough you will surely reap the rewards. But when most of the world's wealth sits in the hands of only a few, whilst the remaining population struggles to live day to day, it's impossible not to question the model we have been born into and continue to feed. We are taught not to question this authority and sadly repeat the cycle by handing over our children at the earliest of ages, programming their minds according to their agenda. We simply conform and believe what we are told, rather than searching for our own truths. We are encouraged to do everything, accept and live according to what will lift us higher. The purpose of this book is to provide the framework for you to move away from this oppression of mind and forge a new way of being that will begin to bring about the life that you desire.

To begin your Success Rebellion journey to a new life, your creativity and your imagination will be essential. You need to be able to see beyond where you are now in order to form a new reality and a new set of circumstances for yourself. When you speak to any high achiever, those who have achieved mass wealth or success, they will all refer to the power of visualisation, which we will discuss later in this chapter. I suggest using visualisation as part of a daily routine in order to reinforce your dream and get you to where you want to be.

As adults we are told that we have to grow up and not dream. We are told to get with the real world. But, personally, I am not happy with the real world. The real world does not serve me or my goals. And so I have to dream. I have to think differently from the rest of society. I have to go against the grain. Otherwise, I risk falling into the same trap, accepting a life that I am not at all happy with.

Really Use Your Skills

To escape entrapment, embrace and use your natural abilities. Begin to identify where your natural skill sets lie. What are your strengths? Where do you excel? You are equipped with talents that are unique to you and you only. When using the gifts that you've been blessed with, do so in a manner that goes beyond just that of your personal needs. An expansion of your awareness will occur as well as the expansion of possibilities. And while it's essential to set your intention, once you've set it, don't be rigid in thought. Be open to all opportunities that arise, as where you first set your intent may not be the best or the final destination for you. And remember that when you dream, sometimes your dreams can be limited to what you can conceive of now. Your dreams will also become more expansive as you grow. Be open to new dreams and allow opportunity to guide you, as fully using your talents will attract the circumstances that will take you higher.

Imagination

The imaginative realm is where all possibilities lie. Within this world you could be as lavish, as big, as bold and as imaginative as you choose to be. There is nothing within the universal realm that cannot be manifested within the physical realm. Therefore, anything that you can conceive of in the mind, you can make a reality. We have lost many of the teachings of the power of imagination, but in recent years, these are starting to come back into light, and we are seeing a shift towards the metaphysical. The teachings of indigenous tribes and cultures are now coming to the forefront and being embraced by the Western world. An example is the West's growing fascination with plant medicine and the shamanic healing ceremonies involving ayahuasca. Escaping their chaotic lives, travelling to the depths of the Amazon rainforest, people just like you and me set out in pursuit of a higher power and want to reconnect to the ancient and universal knowledge that is held and experienced within these sacred ceremonies. There is an inner yearning and desire to discover the depths of their potential, and so their search leads them back to a forgotten world, to the shamans who hold many of the answers they seek.

Within many indigenous tribes, the shaman is the central pillar of the tribe. Shamans perform rituals to break the veil of other realms and other dimensions in order to seek guidance and creative inspiration. They invoke visions and use the messages they receive to provide direction as to what they should do as a tribe. This gives the knowledge of how to better serve their tribe, and they are able to lead the tribe with a clear vision.

Now we see leaders of organisations such as Mark Zuckerberg or the late Steve Jobs, who have created organisations that have sparked from one idea, one vision for a new reality, a new future, a new world. In order to create to the level that they have created or impact the world in such a big way, you first need to be able to see that world in your imagination.

Whatever your goal or your vision, you have to conceive it first within the mind. You have to get clear on it. And then with that clarity you begin to attract the ideas and inspiration that will help you make that vision a reality. You connect in with your sat nav to find your direction. Only then can you begin to attract the thoughts and ideas that help you take action.

The Art of Visualisation

Visualisation is the art of focused thought. We humans have the incredible ability to close our eyes, think of an object or subject and immediately conjure up a mental image or movie to match. So clever and intricate is the human mind that we can also tap into the feelings and emotions that may be associated with that particular image or movie. Just as if you were dreaming, the visualisation becomes very real.

Science has proven that the unconscious mind can't determine between facts and fiction, it simply accepts your thoughts as information and reality. This is one of the reasons why children should not be exposed to violent video games or movies. Their subconscious simply absorbs all that it experiences, and although these acts of violence are contained within a TV screen, the footprint and impressions they leave on these young minds are significant, and sometimes harmful.

Our subconscious mind has the ability to alter our physical body on a molecular level. Once a belief has been formed within the subconscious, it begins to manifest itself in the physical world, whether it be a change in our health, behaviours or actions. Many of us are dreaming victims of our subconscious minds, reactive to the habits and programmes that it has formed. This can sometimes result in negative behaviours and emotions that do not serve our highest good and prevent us from reaching our full potential. However, using visualisation will allow you to regain control of the subconscious and begin using its power for your highest good.

Through the focused awareness of visualisation, you can open the doors of possibility and enrich your world in incredible ways. Through the repetition of carefully considered positive thoughts, it is possible to reprogram the subconscious mind with new beliefs, new stories and new ideas, all of which will manifest themselves in the physical reality, for what the subconscious sees, it believes. And so, through repeated visualisations it must accept that which it is told. Such is its power, that it will begin to attract, inspire and create the stories which it holds, and therefore, if you want to make changes in your world, simply tell yourself a better story. For it is the vehicle of story that unlocks all of life's blessings.

Visualisation is the art of quietening your mind and focusing upon what you want to create, then feeling the emotion of it and experiencing it, as though it were real life. As a result, emotions are sparked that will change how you feel. If you think happy thoughts about what's going on around you, you will begin to feel happy. If you think sad thoughts, and that is where your attention is, then you're automatically going to feel sad. Each time you give energy to a particular feeling, you emit a frequency, which then determines what in you it is going to be attracted to you. If you want to attract mass wealth, you have to begin to feel what it is to be wealthy. You have to truly believe that you have abundance, and you will then attract money. Money attracts money, all because you stood within the vibrational frequency of money. In the same way, when people are in a place of poverty or scarcity generally, they have a scarcity mindset. They are set in a place of lack, and so that is what they attract. If this is you, then you have to change your vibrational frequency. And the way to do this is through the act of visualisation. Create a new reality within your mind's eye and experience the feeling and the emotions that are associated with that, in order to change your vibrational frequency. The higher your frequency, the better the things you'll be attracting within your life.

Top Tips to Create Your New Reality

Visualisation needs to be a daily habit to ensure you reprogram your unconscious. Your unconscious is really about habitual nature. You have to repeat your visualisation over a period of time in order for it to become your new reality.

Dedicate time to visualisation. Take yourself out of your current environment and get out into nature. Walk in the woods. Become grounded and centred in natural space so that you become more connected with your true self.

Think about how you want your future to look. Who do you want to be? Write down this information. Build a picture of your future, a vision of where you want to be and where you deserve to be.

Don't limit your possibilities by putting a time frame on your vision. Many people make the mistake of saying they want to achieve their goals within three or five years; instead allow nature and the universe to help it unfold in front of you. Don't be rushed.

Embrace your Success Rebellion journey, and you'll find it will naturally occur.

A word from Dr John Demartini, one of the world's leading authorities on human behaviour and personal development:

> The magnitude of your vision determines the magnitude of your life. The greater the cause, the greater the vision – and the greater your life.

The more congruent your vision and actions are with your highest values, the broader the vision becomes. And the longer the space and time horizons become, the bigger your vision becomes. A normal worker is going to plan at least day to day. The lower management lives month to month, the middle management year to year, the upper management decade to decade. The CEO lives generation to generation. A visionary lives for a century, and a sage lives for a millennium. So, the magnitude of space and time within one's innermost dominant thought will determine the level of conscious evolution they'll obtain. And their conscious evolution will be in direct proportion to their action steps and their highest values. So, if you are amazingly congruent, your space and time horizons will actually extend, and they'll give rise to more legacies in their creation. Look centuries into the future and hold the vision of what you want to accomplish and think long term.

I'm a firm believer that the magnitude of that vision will determine your outcome in life. You can create a long-term vision, but you have to chunk it down to space and time horizons that you can live in. Chunk it down, and chunk it down into daily actions you can do today that you know will unfold into your vision in the long run. You can't just hold a vision without breaking it down into daily actions that are in line with it and will get the outcome you want.

I love what Dr Demartini is saying: that when your actions and focus are aligned with your vision, an expansion within your awareness occurs, allowing you to see things from a higher plane. No longer do you view life from a hand-to-mouth, day-to-day perspective, but you begin to develop foresight for a bigger and brighter future. The greater your vision, the greater your results. So, if your dreams are to make a huge impact on this planet, then for this to be achieved you must first develop an equally huge vision.

Summary

Creating and maintaining an inspiring vision is essential for motivation and provides you with a clear direction. Your vision will help you to avoid 'average-ism' and protect you from being swept away by the vision of others.

Your vision binds you to the intent of creating a better reality even when the system and your circumstances seem to conspire against you.

By tapping into the realms of the imagination, you can begin manifesting a brighter and better future. Developing a regular practice of focused thought and visualisation will set into motion the wheels of manifestation, helping you to bring your vision into reality.

Reflection

Before you move on to the next chapter take a couple of minutes to think about these questions:

- What is your passion?
- What does happiness look like to you?
- How can you blend these things into your vision and visualisation?

CHAPTER 5

Values

There is no denying that modern-day life has brought much improvement to everyday life. Whether it be the advancements in technology that now grant us the opportunity to click a button and visually communicate with anyone in the world or the ease of being able to ask Alexa absolutely anything and be certain that she will provide a helpful and accurate response. Though these advancements do enhance our lives, there is a flipside, a side of the coin that has a startling effect on our happiness and how we each individually progress in our lives. Technology has infringed on every aspect of our day, competing for our attention and drowning us with so much noise and distraction. It has become an ever-increasing drain on our time and resources, and, as a consequence, we have neglected the bare essentials.

With all that we have now accepted into our lives, we have unconsciously begun to ignore our own inner voice. We no longer hear the call of our inner dialogue. We have become so fixated upon seeking fulfilment from the outside that we spend little to no time learning or familiarising ourselves with who we truly are. I came to this realisation when I was thirty-two and on doing so realised that most of us live within this paradigm. It was one of the biggest learning experiences of my life and came as a result of what I can only describe as a mental blowout or some form of awakening.

I had returned from a two-week trip to Thailand with my fiancée, Justine. Because of jet lag, I was up and into work extra early and was faced with a huge post holiday workload. Having been in relaxation mode for two weeks and then being thrown straight back into the deep end was intense. I was jumping from one task to another just trying to clear the backlog, and my mind was racing at a million miles an hour. On the one hand I felt productive, as I was making the most of the day with the extra early starts, but my energy was so frenetic that after a long day's work I felt like I was in overdrive. On the third day of this routine, I went to bed at around 10:30 but was in a high state of stress. I fell sleep but woke after a few hours in a semi-dream state with my mind running rampant with some crazy and heavy thoughts that were just alien to my normal way of thinking, when a question sprung into my mind. What is consciousness? Then that was it. Boom! That was the trigger that caused a mental explosion. It was as if my mind had imploded and then scattered across the cosmos. That's the only way I can describe it. My mind felt like it had literally been blown open to lay upon the stars. I shot out of my bed with this burning question etched in my mind. This single question kept repeating itself, and I couldn't shake it. It made me question everything I knew. What is reality? What is life? What is this I am experiencing? The enormity of the questions was just too deep for me to handle. I woke Justine, not knowing how to deal with this sudden overwhelming sense of anxiety and fear. It can be difficult to fully understand this experience, and to some extent it is a blessing to be spared the experience, as I wouldn't wish that torment on anyone. But I can only compare the experience to the times of smoking weed, when on the odd occasion you sometimes have that epiphany or a eureka moment, where for a moment you raise your level of consciousness and believe you have either solved or, on a deeper soul level, remembered one of life's mysteries. But as quickly as the discovery comes, it goes, and you are left confused, searching again for that single thought that might yield so many answers. But this night was different; it was as if I had been woken by one of life's big questions, but instead of it escaping back into the ether, the questions stayed with me. The problem was that it was all too much for my mind to comprehend, and so it simply overloaded; that's the only way I can explain it.

For the first time in my life, I was hit with a panic attack. I was struggling to breathe and couldn't stop shaking. The experience was too much for me to deal with. I hoped I would go to sleep and wake up the next day and be fine, but I wasn't. It was like mental torture that stayed with me the next day and for years after. But the traumatic experience did push me to seek the answers to those questions. I began to reconnect with activities that I had ignored since I was a teenager. I moved from one fad to another, trying to escape from the continuous thoughts that plagued me even if it was for just five minutes. I took up golf, fishing and even purchased a set of DJ decks. I believe this was the teaching of the experience, to force me into reconnecting with the essence of who I was and not who I had become. We often hear of people having similar experiences that come under various labels: mental blowouts, breakdowns, and midlife crisis. But through my experience I now believe that these events occur as a result of us living lives in misalignment to who we are. They act as wake-up calls for us to begin a process of soul searching to rediscover the aspects of ourselves that we have neglected or forgotten. It's not that I am destined to be the next superstar DJ or PGA tour winner but more that I remember who I am and what daily experiences and activities lift me higher and realign me to my true path and destiny. So many of us have forgotten who we are and have taken on an identity that doesn't serve our higher self. We no longer remember how to really have fun, and I don't mean getting pissed on the weekend with friends. Many of us have become so disconnected from who we are, that we no longer know what we need to feed our souls.

As your physical body needs nourishment in order for it to perform, so too does your spiritual body, your soul, and its main source of nourishment are positive experiences in accordance with who you are. These experiences make you happier, raising your vibrational frequency, elevating your being and, in turn, lifting you higher. By raising your spiritual vitality you become happier, and you attract even more of what you desire into your daily experience.

These moments of spiritual nourishment are wake-up calls to a more 'values-based way of living' – living in accordance with what you value and who you are. This is something that is essential for every individual. No two sets of values are the same, and they are personal to each and every one of us. I realised that most of us live lives outside of our values. Very few of us dedicate time to the things that truly make us happy. When I speak to friends or to those I meet who complain about their unhappiness in life, lack of fulfilment or progress, very few of them allocate time to a hobby or interests they are truly passionate about. Fun pastimes have become a thing of the past and something they associate with their youth. This is both sad and extremely unhealthy for the mind and soul. And it is a form of self-neglect that can attract some serious repercussions if left unaddressed. It's essential for every man and woman to begin to establish their values so that they can prioritise the experiences, which will provide them with the greatest sense of pleasure and fulfilment and in turn create a happier, more meaningful life, enhancing their state of wellbeing and success.

What Are Values?

To understand my values and to answer the questions of that night, I had to do a lot of reflection and look deep within and honestly ask myself questions that would uncover the truth of who I was. They are questions that are useful for everyone:

- What pastimes do I truly enjoy?
- What experiences feed my soul and bring about a deeper sense of fulfilment?
- What topics of discussion do I naturally gravitate towards?
- What am I passionate about?
- What am I naturally good at, and where do my natural strengths lie?
- What did I enjoy doing when growing up and why?

Through this process of questioning and reflection, I was able to get clarity on who I was and what I should be focusing on. What I now know is that when we live in accordance with our higher values and when we live a life in harmony with that which we value as being important, it brings a greater degree of happiness.

To me, values are not about the airy-fairy stuff that can sometimes have no meaning and that people find difficult to relate to. When I ask someone what their values are and they say honesty or trust, I often think, that's meaningless, and it's just something they've heard someone else say. They are plucking them out of the air, because they have heard someone else say it before them. When I talk about values, I am referring to values that are more about what you value as being truly important in your life. When you ask someone the question – What is important in your life – his or her response is more realistic and tangible and easier to keep track of. If, for example, travelling is something that you really enjoy and it feeds your soul, then if you haven't been travelling for several years, you're neglecting that aspect of yourself, and it's highly likely that this neglect is causing a degree of unhappiness in your life. It's not specifically the travelling that we value, but what comes out of the travelling experience that really matters – connecting with new people, experiencing new cultures and new foods, being in the moment and being spontaneous and getting out of your everyday routines. These may be the reasons why you enjoy travelling or the freedom associated with it. Only by incorporating that within your life will you be serving yourself to the highest level. This is why I approach values from a different and more practical perspective.

Because the things you value have a positive impact on your life, it's important to ensure they feature in your life. To do this they need to be:

- Actionable
- Measurable
- Give control to your life

ACTIONABLE

Once you have decided what your values are, you have to take action to include them in your life, so that you can move towards what is important to you. If your value is actionable, then you will be able to take easy steps to start redesigning your life. You don't want to have to reach for the impossible or unachievable, as you will soon lose motivation. By knowing you can take actions, no matter how small, you will grow in confidence, self-esteem and have a sense of achievement that will keep you focused on your journey.

MEASURABLE

Taking travelling again as an example, you know how many holidays you've booked in for the year. It's very easy for you to measure whether you have been successful in achieving this value.

If your value is connecting with your family or friends you'll want to dedicate time to spend with those you care about most. You can measure this easily by looking at your call history and identifying who and how many friends and family you have spoken to over the past week. You can check your diary over the last three months to determine how many days or evenings you've dedicated to socialising with friends. And if you have not spent enough time on the things you value, then make time and space in your diary so that you do spend time with the people you love. These are quantifiable values. In summary, values have to be measureable so that you can actually see the impact of the actions you are taking.

GIVE CONTROL TO YOUR LIFE

The things you value are like your pillars. They set the boundaries for your behaviour. All of the decisions we make as people are based upon our values. So whenever we're stuck or we're unsure as to what decision to make or how we should approach a particular situation, we refer to our values. Once we know our values, we will get clarity on the decision we should make as an individual. Whenever you are unsure as to how you should proceed, you can revert to your values. They will give you the guidance to make the right decision for you.

Values in the Business Setting

In the corporate world, values can be superficial. Some organisations do not give establishing their values the time and effort they deserve. They choose values such as trustworthiness or professionalism based on what they think sounds good to their customer rather than who they actually are as a company.

No matter where you work, whether you are an employee in an organisation or you are an entrepreneur, those business values should reflect who you are as an individual. Therefore, if you are an employee, there should be similarities between your values and those of the company you work for. Or if you are an entrepreneur, you will want the values of your business to represent who you are as a person. We have to be true to who we are, whether that is in our own personal lives or in work situations. If you work for companies that have similar values to you, you will stay excited about your job or the business you have set up. One of the key factors that drives us as humans is our sense of community, our sense of belonging. When you find that you are working in an organisation that doesn't reflect who you are, you will find a lack of synergy between your values and that of the organisation and become demotivated as a result. If you are sacrificing your time to contribute to the success of this organisation and they don't reflect your values, it is going to affect your sense of belonging and ultimately your happiness. That is why I recommend you do your research on the company you think you would like to work for. Find out if they will truly reflect who you are as a person before you apply, and only go for the job if their values as a company resonate with your own.

Values and Vision

We discussed in the previous chapter the importance of having a vision for the future. We introduced the concept of visualisation in order for you to start tapping into the metaphysical world and the Law of Attraction. To do this you have to be a higher-vibration being. That means you have to do what makes you happy and live in accordance with your values.

Your vision and values go hand in hand; there must be synergy between the two. Your vision and values must be in harmony with one another to be successful. Anything less is just sending conflicting messages to the universe, which will be reflected in your experience. I know many people whose values contradict their vision. Don't forget, it is your values that drive your behaviour, and so it's very easy to develop a vision for the future, but be committed to a set of values that take you away from where you want to be.

Values and Self-Governance

From Chapter 1 you'll remember that self-governance is about free thinking. It is about thinking for yourself. But in order for you to think for yourself, you actually have to know who you are. To do that, you have to know what your values are – who you are as an individual and what you stand for in this world. Maya Angelou says that 'You must first understand where you come from in order to know where you are going'. It's not so much about where you were born but more the roots of who you are, the essence of your nature, and your values define that essence.

Values go deep. They are personal. When someone thinks of you as an individual, what would they say about you? Our values distinguish us from each other. You, therefore, have to know what you represent. This is vital to self-governance. You have to know who you are, what is right for you and what isn't.

But our values don't always stay the same. What we value as being important changes as we grow as individuals. My values are different to what they were ten years ago. Now I have a family. And I'm embarking on a deep spiritual journey. Consequently, what I value as being important has changed as I've grown and as I've experienced life. You have to be open to that change too. Often true friendship can be revealed when someone has a change or when a big life event occurs. When a friend has a child, it's likely to change their values. Before that they may have partied and socialised regularly. They formed their relationships based on those values, but at the point when they have a child, that value may then change. This gives a good indication as to the strengths of those relationships, because it's highly likely that a lot of those people that you once connected with solely because of the partying will slowly start to fall by the wayside, and only your true friends will then be left.

This change happens across all areas of your life – your friendships and your relationships with your family and your partner. It is important to brace yourself for what may come about as a result of living more aligned with your values or when it comes to changes in your values, but I guarantee you will be a much happier and much more fulfilled person as a result.

Identifying Your Values

By values, I mean those of a higher vibrational frequency, values of a positive nature that uplift as opposed to having an adverse effect. There are, of course, many things that you may value as being important, but the distinction to be made is focusing your efforts on the values that take you forward as opposed to pulling you back. Consequently, establishing your values takes a period of reflection and looking at what it is that you enjoy. You need to identify your wants and passions, and you can do this through thinking about the conversations you enjoy, looking at how you spend your time and identifying the common ground you have with friends.

We have talked previously in this chapter about the value of community, of friendships and socialising, but it is important to understand the people you are connecting with need to share the same values as you. Look at their social feeds. What do they post about? From just scrolling through someone's social feed, you can learn a lot about his or her values. This will help you identify your values too, because you gravitate towards that which you desire and that which you value. By looking across your social feeds you will get an indication of what you naturally gravitate towards.

When you think about socialising with your friends, what do you talk about when you're out with them? What are the topics of conversation when you're at home with your partner? How do you spend your money? That is a great way to identify your values. On a monthly basis, check your bank statement to identify where your money is going, and that will give you a good indication of what you value in your life.

My Philosophy

Understanding my own values brought me to my realisation about what was important to me. Finding my values came from my journey, my personal growth and an increased understanding of what I wanted from life. That is why, in this chapter, I have given you the simplest approach to identifying your values.

I have three key values that are important to my life and who I am today:

- My family
- Personal and spiritual development
- Being of service sharing my knowledge and expertise

Family is the most important value to me. Once I had children, they became my life. I don't go out as much as I did, hardly ever, in fact. When I finish work, I go home. I'm generally either working or with my family – that's it. But in my twenties my outlook was very different, and my values were more about materialism. I thought who you were seen with, who you were friends with and how others perceived you were the things that were important, and I based a lot of friendships upon that. I was driven by ego and material possessions and sacrificed many of my values in the attainment of that. However, I am now able to see things from a much broader prospective.

One of the biggest catalysts for this change in my outlook is my commitment to personal and spiritual development. I love learning about new and exciting life philosophies, practices and strategies that have the potential to help me enhance my life experience. I love learning about indigenous cultures and ancient traditions that provide an insight to our true nature and purpose here on earth. My outlook is to become a better version of myself each day, continuously improving in order to become all that I can be. And there is no better feeling in this world than when I am able to share this newfound knowledge and insight to empower others to make positive changes within their lives, taking them towards where they want to be. I see the world from a somewhat different perspective from those around me, so I enjoy sharing my wisdom. There's a sense of nourishment that happens when you're participating in what you truly value. When I'm sharing information, it's feeding my soul. When I'm growing, it's feeding my soul. Your values should feed your soul too.

Making a difference, being able to impact others and the world in a greater way. That's what I truly value now. Whereas before, I just cared about me, myself and I, and what the world could give me, as opposed to what I could give the world. Now, wanting to help others is what drives me. My personal growth and development is focused on how I can be of service to others.

Summary

The values we live by start with us. They are the essence of what makes us who we are. They are what is important to us in our lives. When we lack clarity in our values, we become unfulfilled and unhappy.

Take the time to think about what is important to you. Think about conversations you enjoy having, the things you like to do, and who you want to spend your time with. These are good indicators of your values.

Once you establish your key values, make sure they are actionable, measurable and give control to your life. Once you start to take action to move your life towards what is important to you, you will find that sense of purpose in your life that you have been searching for.

Reflection

Before you move onto the next chapter take a few minutes to think about the following:

- Identify the values that are important to you.
- How do they relate to your vision: Do your values compliment your vision for the future?

CHAPTER 6

Beliefs

From the outside looking in, those who have acquired mass wealth or have risen to exponential heights may seem to possess some form of superhuman powers. Their achievements seem to defy all logic, with their success reaching beyond the capabilities of normal man. We sit and wonder how they manoeuvred their way to the top, how they found their inspiration, and how they acquired the courage that set them on their way. No different than the old Greek legends such as Achilles and Apollo, the names of these modern-day cult heroes will become immortalised by their triumphs. And an air of mystique grows to surround them. We make the mistake of placing these individuals on pedestals, as though they have something to offer the world that you and I don't. We unconsciously categorise them and their success in a place that's out of our reach.

However, it's not superhuman strength or psychic skills that separates their achievement from ours; it is simply a small shift in thought, that once developed or nurtured, will empower us to become the masters of our own universe. Those who do great things, the game changers, the elite performers, are able to do what they do time and time again because of one very simple reason: they believe they can.

When we strip away the façade and look into the very core of those who have impacted the world in a big way, one common thing separates them from their fellow man. Despite being only human, despite their normality, they've harnessed the one essential attribute that has propelled them to huge success in their careers. They've harnessed the infinite power of their beliefs: belief in themselves, their vision, and in their life's work and mission for a bigger and better future. Those who dare to believe are the ones who push the boundaries of normality and etch their names into the history books forever. And for you: if you can harness your beliefs as they do, there is nothing that you cannot do.

How to Change Your World

Knowing this key principle gives you the ability to instantly change your world, catapulting you onto your Success Rebellion journey right now. Your beliefs can either make or break you. It's crucial that you learn to become aware of your own personal belief system, because your beliefs can be detrimental to your future happiness. They have the ability to either empower you or disempower you. When we form negative beliefs, they can act as shackles that keep us down and hold us back from achieving prosperity and good fortune.

When we come into this world, we arrive free of any prior conditional beliefs. We are pure in every sense of the word. From the moment of our birth we enter a stage of discovery, and up until the age of seven we are in our most impressionable stage for learning and the adoption of beliefs. Our beliefs begin to form mainly as a result of our parents' influence at first, and then later at school, from our teachers, friends, family and wider society. Throughout time, there has always been some form of external influence that has shaped the way we see the world – whether that be governments, religion, community or just local culture – however, we are now in an era where the control over how we think, feel and behave is diminishing by the day, with little protection against the external influences that threaten to manipulate our very being. With the advancement of technology, we are indoctrinated with beliefs from every angle through the medium of news, advertising, TV programmes, social networks and films. They are rarely positive and serve the purpose of limitation and control only. What is worrying about this is that we take on the beliefs from the world around us and accept them as our own.

But here's the real news: you don't have to accept other people's beliefs as the truth, making them your own reality. You can create new beliefs for yourself, and for the rest of the world. In years past, it was a universally held belief that the capacity for flight was exclusive to the birds. So, too, was it believed that we inhabited a flat earth and sailors would perish if they ventured too close to the world's edge. Despite the general consensus of thinking that certain things were impossible, some individuals decide to not adopt this collective thought. Instead, they imposed their own will on this world, and in doing so they changed the planet as we know it.

Confucius said it best: 'Those who think they can and those who think they can't are usually both right'. If we believe we can do something, we will gravitate towards it and take action to do it. If we don't believe we can do it, we resist even trying. Your beliefs underpin your perception on the world. But with a change in belief comes a change in your world. And then we can move on it.

The Unseen World

The world is at a crucial point in its evolution, with an ever-increasing awareness of all things metaphysical. Metaphysical being the intangible, the things we cannot see or physically sense. Within this shift in awareness, more and more information is being shared and taught on the power of our thoughts and beliefs. The fact that we possess the ability to create our circumstances through our beliefs or thoughts can be a difficult concept to comprehend. But if you were to place your life under scrutiny, it would reveal that most of what you have currently created in your life was, at one point, all that you ever wanted. And so in effect, unknowingly, you have already participated in the art of attraction and creation.

Unfortunately, it's that continuous need for more and participation in this consumerist world that keeps us in a feeling of lack. We never feel as though we're actually winning. However, if you were to tally up your scorecard over the past ten years and reflect upon your accomplishments, the results may surprise you. What can also affect your attitude towards the power of your beliefs is that past life experience tells you something very different. For as long as you can remember, you may have dreamt of living a lavish life, big cars, big houses and all of the trappings of wealth and fortune. You then hear me say, it is all possible if you simply believe.

But you've wanted this for years, and none of the above has presented itself in any shape or form, and your life is pretty much the same as it's always been. The reason you have not yet attracted this change of circumstances is that although you may consciously say that you believe, the possessions that you want and the change that you seek can be so far removed from your current reality that your unconscious beliefs have demonstrated something very different. Your core beliefs are buried deep within your subconscious, and so simply desiring a particular object or circumstance is not enough. You must learn to believe it with every part of your being. You must learn how to influence your inner belief system for the better so you can begin to change your outer experience for the good.

When studying the success stories of others, in any setting, the number one characteristic that is evident within each individual is their personal beliefs. Their personal beliefs about themselves and their ability to achieve huge success in what they do. Don't assume they were born with these characteristics. Quite often they have developed over time, building up bit by bit, as all it takes is one key event to totally change your perspective forever. It's never too late for you to change your paradigm, so don't be disheartened if you feel as though age is not your ally, as once this shift has occurred, the bounty of life is yours to immediately tap into.

Beliefs are one of the fundamental keys to success, so take time to reflect on your current belief system. What are your beliefs around yourself? What do you believe about your self-worth? And how about money, action or work rate? If you believe in abundance, you will achieve abundance. If you believe that you have to work hard for twenty hours a day in order to achieve success, then this will be so. Study the beliefs of those who are where you want to be, the wealthy, the successful, and the happy. What you believe becomes your reality. So if your beliefs do not serve you, change them. It's quite simple.

As part of the research for this book I interviewed key experts to find out their expert views. On the subject of beliefs, Dr Bruce H. Lipton, PhD, best-selling author and stem cell biologist told me:

> If your subconscious mind was programmed growing up in a rich family, then you'll have acquired a program of how to make money. You don't even have to focus on it; you just download it as an infant. You are already learning how to make money by observing your family and how they do it. And if you come from a poor family, your subconscious programming is likely to support the view that life is a struggle, and no matter what

> you do, no matter how hard you work you're still going to be poor. So, it's the subconscious programming (your beliefs) that determines whether you're going to be rich or poor, without your conscious mind even being involved; you receive the programming beforehand. If someone grew up in a family that made money, they will unconsciously seek making money, but they may not consciously understand what the heck they are doing, if it's not coming from consciousness; it's just subconscious automatic behaviour.

Dr Bruce H. Lipton explains that much of who you are is as a result of the programming and learned behaviour you inherited as a child from your parents and those around you. History often repeats itself, so to establish a new outcome you have to break the habits of old, literally rewiring the subconscious mind to form new beliefs that reflect the future you want to create.

My Learning

In my earlier years I had no dreams, little to no ambition and no hope for a brighter future. My environment defined me, and so I succumbed to its gravitational pull. A few weeks before my eighteenth birthday I felt a growing sense of excitement. It marked a huge milestone in my life, but the excitement wasn't for the reason you would normally expect for such a significant point in my life. For some people, when hitting this symbolic age, their excitement comes from the joy of being able to finally go to the pub or a bar with friends and get drunk. For some, it may be that they are finally of an age where they can legally have a tattoo. For others it could be the fact they can now vote, for which many hundreds of thousands if not millions have sacrificed their lives for this opportunity.

But for me, my reasoning was not so meaningful. My excitement derived from the fact that I was now of an age to claim jobseekers' allowance. WOW! How crazy is that? At this time in my life my source of happiness came from being eligible to claim just £40 per week in government handouts, and the crazy thing is I actually thought I was winning. I had accepted the belief that £40 was my value in this world, and the sad thing was that I was quite happy with that belief.

It wasn't until I started broadening my horizons, trying new experiences outside of my normal environment and enabling my own personal development that my beliefs about myself started to change. I developed a new understanding of what was actually possible and what I could become. I have changed my beliefs by being the creator of new experiences. I have transformed the landscape of my world and truly believe I can do and be whoever and whatever I choose. I now own a thriving business, have been nominated for various national business awards and turn over millions of pounds each year. Recently, I completed a luxury villa development in Asia just for the simple fact that I wanted to and knew I could. And at the end of the book I share details of my current project with you too. Now my focus is stepping into my real life work, the good shit I'm here to do, and so, as I write this book, I am in the planning stages of developing a unique wellness resort concept that is set to revolutionise the wellbeing industry. A far cry from signing on for my £40 per week but no better example of how your life can change as soon as you begin to change your beliefs of what is truly possible.

You can too, by being the creator of your own experiences, which in turn will result in changing your negative beliefs that are keeping you stuck and unable to change your life for the better.

Change Your Beliefs

I want to give you easy ways to change your beliefs and start the process of embarking on your own personal development journey. However, the first key point to understand is that you can't just remove beliefs. You have to form new ones. The definition of madness is doing the same thing over and over again and expecting different results. Therefore, one of the key ways to change your belief system is to create new experiences. That way you will start to form new thoughts, new emotions and new patterns of behaviour. Do things you wouldn't normally do to break your normal routines of behaviour. Commit to a new activity. Choose random ones, stepping outside of your comfort zone rather than something predictable. I've had a random desire to visit the opera. This is a totally different world to what I'm used to and wouldn't be something that I would generally gravitate towards. However, I know – and it's probably why I am experiencing the urge – that as a result of attending and immersing myself in this cultured environment, it will expose me to a new experience and subsequently cause me to form new neurological pathways, leading to a shift in my beliefs. By taking yourself out of your comfort zone and repeating the process again and again, you can start to break that cycle of low achieving and start forming new and more positive routines.

There are three key ways to start to change your beliefs:

- Setting small goals
- Using affirmations
- Reflecting to enhance learning

SETTING SMALL GOALS

A belief is a repeated thought. In order to break the cycle, you have to begin to think differently and reinforce these positive thought patterns with a succession of small wins. Set goals and objectives that are within your reach. If you haven't already developed the art of this principle, it's always best to start with the low-hanging fruit, otherwise you will inevitably set yourself up for failure. Choose small goals first; gain momentum and confidence in the process. Then when you begin to experience the success of this principle, you can push the boundaries, becoming more imaginative in your desires.

USING AFFIRMATIONS

Affirmations alone are not enough to change your beliefs. There has to be something behind an affirmation to give it that extra energetic charge. That stems from your emotions and your intent. Emotions are energy in motion. To begin forming new beliefs, you have to support those affirmations with the vibrational frequency of the feeling or intention of the words. Without this emotional energy, an affirmation is just words. Once you add the emotion, it amplifies its intent. It is this amplification that helps forge your new belief system as new neurological pathways are created within the brain. Repetition of this process strengthens these pathways until they become your new default setting. Science refers to this process as 'neuroplasticity', with the brain being able to continuously form new neurons (nerve cells) when given new instruction or direction.

REFLECTING TO ENHANCE LEARNING

True learning only comes with reflection. When doing an activity, an exercise or training, we're consciously immersed in that act. But it's not until we step outside of that process that we actually see the consequence of what we have been doing. When you're in the gym, the growth comes after your exercise when you're sleeping or resting and your muscles repair and rebuild themselves. The same applies to personal development or your work. When you are learning or working, you are so busy that you don't necessarily see what has really occurred. You are looking at it from a micro level. You have to take a step out and see the bigger picture. That is why when you go on holiday, it's a great time for reflection, because you're not caught up in your thinking. You have the opportunity to look at your job from a wider perspective.

Safeguard Your Beliefs

Once you begin to change what you believe about yourself, you need to ensure that these new positive beliefs remain installed in your mind and safeguard them so that they become part of your very being. Life will always give rise to new challenges, which can work against you, so be on guard.

Three of these key challenges are:

- Negative self-talk
- Social media
- Materialism

NEGATIVE SELF-TALK

Is who you are in alignment with what you believe? How do you see yourself? Where do you want to go in your life? Who do you want to be? Sometimes our self-talk is in conflict with the vision we have of ourselves. Think about how many times you say you can't afford a particular thing. This thinking allows feelings of scarcity to creep in and cause conflict with the beliefs you want to instil about yourself and your future. Self-talk like this can be a sign that you are resisting the new belief you want to develop. In this case, you may have to do a deeper level of work to clear that old baggage out and to embrace the new ideas about yourself that you want to adopt. You have to be conscious of what you say and make sure that there is that alignment with who you want to be. My advice is to use affirmations in order to override this.

SOCIAL MEDIA

Jim Rohn, the godfather of personal development, says that you have to stand guard at the door of your mind, which means that you need to be conscious about what you expose yourself to. I believe that social media can either empower or disempower you. If you focus on negativity or ideas that are not conducive to the world that you want to create for yourself, then you must gain control over that. I notice this when looking at my social media stream. So many negative posts can drain my energy and lower my vibrational frequency. With social media it is crucial to be disciplined enough to take ownership over your state of being. Be mindful of what serves you and what doesn't, and only allow into your experience those things that are going to lift you higher. Consciously take responsibility for this. Use social media to raise, not lower, your vibrational frequency. And this applies to external stimuli such as TV too. Or it could even be relationships, friends or family members, as we've discussed previously. Negative people can leave you drained, demotivated, even demoralised. These individuals are no longer worthy of your company. And it is not that I'm saying that you're better than them. But you have a responsibility to yourself so take control and safeguard yourself, your future and the life that you want to create.

MATERIALISM

Refuse to get sucked into materialistic desires. Understand the difference between necessity and want, need and desire. Have strength in who you are and in your vision. Be aware of self-governance, but adopt balance according to where you're at and where you want to be. If you have difficulty managing that, then eliminate possible distractions.

For example, unsubscribe to newsletters that draw you into the upcoming sale with a 25% discount. Unfollow those on your social media accounts whose lifestyles and spending make you feel inadequate as you are. Be practical, but always put yourself first, structuring your life according to where you're at and your strengths and weaknesses, and put the necessary safeguards in place so materialism doesn't distract you from where you want to be.

Ever-Changing Beliefs

Now you've started to change your beliefs and know that safeguarding those new, positive beliefs is essential to becoming the person you want to be, you probably think your work is done. But this is just the start of your journey, because your beliefs are ever changing, and you'll need to apply the strategies you've learned in this chapter time and time again to stay on track to being who you want to be.

Remember how I told you how little I valued myself when I was eighteen years old? How I believed that I was worth no more than a mere £40 a week? Well, I've come a long way since then. I've changed my life by changing the beliefs I had about myself.

But here is the thing: those beliefs continuously change as we develop and grow and as we create new experiences for ourselves. I continue to challenge myself to change my beliefs, if necessary. As I shared earlier in the chapter, recently I've been thinking about going to the opera for the first time. I want to understand the music, the minds of those amazing composers, and learn more about how music has the ability to influence us on a deep, unconscious level. But there's more I want from this new experience. I've held a long-standing belief that I don't belong in such an environment, mixing with the types that might attend the Royal Opera House. Am I worthy enough to step inside the world of such establishments and mix with a social class different from my own? Well, it's time to change that belief. Time to widen my palette of experience in order for me to grow and become more. Going to the opera is a million miles away from what those around me would probably choose to do. It will take me out of my comfort zone and put me in a different environment with different people. BUT in doing so, it will trigger those neurological pathways opening up my mind to a new perspective. And that is what this is really all about. Opening a new perspective: bringing in new and different people, new conversations, new thought systems that I can tap into, so that the belief I used to hold about myself will be replaced by a new and positive belief that I am absolutely where I should be the night I take my seat in the Royal Opera House. This new experience will raise my frequency and allow me to tap into the collective thought and opportunities that are usually perceived to be exclusive to this social class.

You can do this too. Take action to identify the negative beliefs you hold about yourself. Be a creator of new experiences. Enable yourself to move out of your comfort zone into new unknown territory to grow personally and to form new beliefs that will allow you to become the person you want to be.

Summary

Your beliefs can be harmful to your present and future happiness. Negative beliefs will hold you back from achieving all that you want in your life. But you can change your beliefs by creating new experiences for yourself. In doing do, you break your patterns of behaviour that have kept you stuck and prevented you from moving forward.

There are three key ways to start to change your beliefs:

- Setting small goals
- Using affirmations
- Reflection to enhance learning

Using all three of these together will enable you to change what you believe about yourself, but added to this, you will need to ensure that once your new belief is installed, you safeguard it against factors such as:

- Negative self-talk
- Social media
- Materialism

By guarding against these influences, you'll clear the way for new beliefs to become part of your being.

Your beliefs are constantly changing. As you grow more as a person, you will find that your beliefs change and evolve according to the experiences you create. Allow them to flow to you and welcome them in.

Reflection

Before you move onto the next chapter take a few minutes to think about the following:

- What is the key belief you need to change in order to move towards the life you want to have?
- What experience can you create to begin to change that belief?
- What is the new belief you want to form about yourself as a result of that experience?

CHAPTER 7

Connection

There has been a long-standing battle between religion and science, with either side having a conflicting understanding of the world and our place within it. The foundations of most religious principles are that we are here by design and have been created to form part of a greater plan, with each religion baring reference to a mystical higher power that demonstrates its divine force through miracles and unexplained phenomena, converting its followers.

While science has advanced the theory that life and creation occurred by chance, and thus it is not a divine force but evolution over a period of many thousands of years that is responsible for the creation of the world that we know. The scientific approach is based on tangible evidence, as mysticism has no place in the scientific world.

However, it seems we have now reached a point in time where there may be space for both religion and science to coexist. Through the field of metaphysics, for the first time, science is able to corroborate many of the teachings of spirituality in relation to the supernatural or unexplained forces that have the capacity to perform miracles with healing, manifestation and other psychic phenomena.

Most religious texts give reference to a universal life force that connects and flows through all things. Depending on your faith, it may be referred to as spirit, nature or matter. Its label isn't important, but your understanding of it and the relevance it has to your life, is.

The energy that I have come to experience through my growth is energy that connects to all life and all things. Everything here on earth exists as a result of its relationship with this energy. Its connectedness means that everything impacts the other, therefore, any change and movement has a knock-on effect on the rest of the planet. Scientists have referred to this as the butterfly effect, meaning that the smallest of changes – such as the flapping of butterfly's wings – within complex systems can cause effects elsewhere in the system. Motion can create a domino effect, with even a subtle movement triggering a series of events that could eventually build the motion that could cause a hurricane on the other side of the planet.

With this in mind, it shows us just how, through this web of invisible energy that connects all things, the most insignificant of actions may in fact have a much larger impact that we can ever know. From this new understanding there are three key areas that you must pay particular attention to, as learning to strengthen your connection with each will make you healthier, happier and will help you to gain clarity on your significance in this world:

- Nature
- Each other
- The metaphysical

NATURE

Nature has provided us with all that we need in order to live our best lives. From food, fresh water, medicine and raw materials, we have been provided with a full panoply of items that have been perfectly designed solely for our benefit. Yet in our arrogance, the Western world has come to a point in our evolution where it is as though we believe that we can do better, and so have snubbed nature's offerings and chosen to take our own route, operating mostly outside of nature. Everything we do reflects where we actually are as a society. Small things, like walking barefoot, couldn't be a more natural process, but if you were to walk down your local high street without footwear, passers-by would consider you crazy. You would be judged, when really it is the behaviour of the masses that should be questioned. I've witnessed mothers being frowned upon because they breastfeed their child in public, by people who would prefer to see the child feed from a cold plastic inanimate bottle rather than feed from their mum. Yet it's likely that these same people would be delighted to see newborn puppies suckling from their mum. 'But they are animals', I hear you say. Yes, you are right – they are – but so are we!

We wonder why there is an increasing number of people experiencing displacement within the 'modern world'. This stems from how we now live: the foods we eat, the things we desire, generally, are from unnatural sources. We have completely broken the natural order and have come away from what we were intended to be, losing our sense of our roots in the process. We have mostly disassociated ourselves from the natural world and therefore have surrendered much of the wellbeing, knowledge and wisdom that are available to us when living in accordance with nature. Early inhabitants of our world had a special relationship with their environment and their natural surroundings, which brought them an abundance of life, health and prosperity, far different from what we see today. Our focus was on building the connection, that relationship with nature, and then nurturing it. However, the powers-that-be had a different agenda for us. They sold us a lifestyle that has moved away from a natural state of being, so that they could sell us products, which by the way, we had to work harder to pay for. Therefore, today we focus on the material world and the tangible products of society and consumerism. That is now our focus. We've forgotten what it is to live in harmony with our natural environment. And we suffer from the consequences, through ill health and a general lack of wellbeing.

Another example is the wearing of sunglasses. With approximately 1.2 million known species of animals on the planet, we are the only species who deem it necessary to cover our eyes to protect us from a perceived danger from the sun's rays.

However, I would argue that this popular fashion accessory may cause more harm than good, as it limits over 1500 wavelengths of light that help regulate the human body's biology, including the production of melatonin that is known to regulate sleep and help suppress cancer growth within the body.

Our ancestors had an entirely different relationship with the sun. Many ancient civilisations including the Aztecs and ancient Egyptians practiced the art of sungazing, where at particular times of the day when there were considered to be no UV rays, they would gaze at the sun. Such practice is said to remove the need for food as you are able to access energy directly from the sun. It is also said to have provided huge improvements in physical and emotional health, providing healing throughout the body as well as raising their level of consciousness. Still, today we have yogis who teach this ancient practice, such as Hira Ratan Manek, who has undergone rigorous trials by top American universities in collaboration with NASA and has demonstrated the wonders of this ancient practice.

Wearing sunglasses whenever there is a hint of sunshine is yet another example of how we place our fashion needs in front of what our body needs to be healthy.

We forget that nature is perfectly designed for us. It can provide us with anything that we need to flourish and survive. When we live in accordance with nature, we can only live a life of optimum vitality and wellbeing.

EACH OTHER

As human beings, we see ourselves as being separate from everything and everyone. Our focus is so much upon our own differences that we no longer look to find what binds us, what connects us with one another. In the space of just a few decades, community has been destroyed with hardly any of us knowing the names of our neighbours, let alone conversing with them on a regular basis. A growing rise in fear, poor work-life balance, TV, social platforms, e-commerce and the fast pace of our lives have all contributed to how little we genuinely interact with one another, to the extent that it seems that everything has been set up to separate us from one another and to dislike ourselves in our natural state.

There is one particular social platform that would like us to believe that we live more connected lives. But I would say that a phone or computer screen cannot replace genuine face-to-face interaction with others. Connecting with others is inherent to who we are as a species. Is it any wonder that the 'psychiatric disorders' many doctors refer to involve some disruption of normal social behaviour? This highlights the importance of regular social interaction. There is a clear direct link between forming social connections and the hormone oxytocin, also referred to as the happy or cuddle hormone. Oxytocin is produced naturally in the body, but levels have been found to increase when social connections are formed, and we generally see higher levels of oxytocin present in individuals with stronger social bonds. Research and studies show oxytocin reduces depression, stress and anxiety and improves overall happiness and mental wellbeing. Our goal as human beings has to be to rekindle the relationship we once had with one another, and in doing so we naturally begin to uplift our own personal wellbeing.

METAPHYSICAL

One of the key pillars of ancient cultures and civilizations was their connection with the spirit realm or the unseen and the intangible. That was the focal point of their society. Their connection with unseen realms brought them a deeper understanding of their purpose and the role they were here to play on earth. These pillars bound each individual together. What is clear is that the knowledge held by these ancient cultures far exceeds what we know today, with much of the information either being suppressed or downplayed. In modern times, many of the spiritual practices held by indigenous tribes are documented as being evil, devil worship or given some form of negative connotation. Terms such as 'black magic' were coined to create fear and unease in the minds of those who were alien to these cultures. But if we were to revert back to the origins of most religions, we would see their roots heavily embedded in the spiritual practices, and so we must give greater respect to these cultures and reconnect with their knowledge and the relationship they had with the unseen.

Our current focus is on the tangible. We only believe what we can see and no longer believe in the magic of life. We've lost that belief, because we're no longer of that frequency and in that mindset. We need to strengthen our connections in all of these three areas above. Exploring this and following a spiritual journey will lead you to have a greater understanding, giving you a vantage point and the tools and knowledge required to truly live an impactful life in accordance with who you inherently are.

By re-establishing the connections with these three aspects you then begin to move back into your natural form as God or nature intended. We, unfortunately, weren't built with a manual, but much of the knowledge and wisdom of who we are already sits within us. It is for us to remember what and who our true being really is. Only then will you slowly start to uncover your true power and your majesty. You will begin to tap into the innate ability and intuitive nature that can guide you through life and the challenges that you experience. This happens when you start to establish or reconnect with who you are.

Indigenous Cultures

Ironically, in order to sustain our modern way of being we need to increase our understanding of the past. We can learn much from our ancestors' connection with nature and their relationship with it. They knew that nature's true essence was bountiful and that it would provide a continuous supply if treated in the right way. When making a killing or a sacrifice, it was done with the greatest or the highest of intent and always in a sustainable way.

The majority of medicines, traditional and Western, are derived from ingredients from plants and trees, knowledge of which came from the teachings of indigenous tribesmen or shamans who shared this wisdom with the Western world. I believe that these people are the true wardens of the planet, because they have respect for the bounty it provides us with, especially food. When you think of a Native American or Aborigine, you might believe their teachings and their culture to be primitive and based on superstition. But as you begin to explore and understand their culture in greater depth, you realise that a lot of their rituals and ceremonies actually serve a far greater purpose, one that is beyond the awareness of an average Westerner. These teachings are the foundation of who you are, and if you were to retrace your lineage it would, undoubtedly, track back to a traditional way of living, though it would differ according to your culture and country. It's essential that as humanity further evolves, we do not totally disregard the teachings of our ancestors. Our ancestors are our teachers.

Indigenous cultures made better connections because their relationships were heart-centred. They were true. They were present in the moment. They dedicated time for connection and formed genuine relationships and learning. The sense of community within these tribes is unparalleled, with everybody contributing to the greater good of the tribe as opposed to individual needs.

They had a better connection with the metaphysical too. Their spirituality underpins their lives, in everything they do. In our world, technology has taken over and become the object of our attentions, whereas the central pillars or foundations of indigenous communities provide a sense of belonging, that sense of purpose, that sense of why and that sense of reason. These pillars give the answers to why we are here. What is the purpose of life? What is the purpose of experience? They provided answers that many people are now seeking, because they can't find the answers in the distractions around them. They know that there's more to life, but they haven't found out what that is yet. Within indigenous cultures, there was a connection with divinity. It was the building block for their way of life and gave meaning to their existence. Divinity provided and helped to bind that community within a set of values and a life philosophy that honoured who they were.

The Separation from Nature

NATURAL BEINGS LIVING WITHIN UNNATURAL HABITATS

We live in an artificial world – natural beings living in an unnatural habitat. Look around you. What can you see? There is nothing more unnatural than organic beings living in the confines of a concrete metropolis, with few trees, drinking treated water from plastic bottles, consuming processed foods bombarded with electromagnetic waves to heat them and working without access to daylight. This is the daily routine for the general population. The modern world we've created isn't conducive to who we are as organic beings.

Fortunately, we are becoming more aware of the consequences of our choices. For example, we now know the long-term negative health effects of consuming artificial and processed foods. It's surprising what a difference even a few days makes to those who eliminate their artificial, convenience-food diets and switch to a cleaner, organic-based lifestyle. They report huge surges in energy, vitality and overall wellbeing.

What many of us fail to realise is that we are energetic beings, operating at a particular frequency. In order for us to be healthy, we have to be in harmony with nature's frequency. Consuming unnatural foods lowers our frequency and vibration and has an unnatural effect on our being, causing an array of side effects, which show up in ill health and disease.

It doesn't stop with the food and drink we consume, but quite literally anything and everything that we are exposed to affects us. Any repeated external stimuli not of a natural vibration would have a disharmonious effect on how we function as human beings. Music, sound and light all affect us on some level.

It is so easy to kid ourselves into believing that we aren't animals and so are separate from the rest of the animal kingdom. But if we were ever thrown into an environment where we didn't have access to a hairbrush or nail clippers, shaving utensils or clothes, it would soon become evident how connected we are to the natural animal kingdom.

Impact of the Separation from Nature

We are now seeing the impacts of this separation from nature materialising in disease, mental health and alcohol problems.

DISEASE

Pesticides, sugars, artificial foods, drink and cigarettes create inflammation and mucus in the body, creating illness and disease. Our bodies run well, energetically, with the right fuel. But just as an unleaded petrol car isn't built to run on diesel fuel, we are not designed to run on artificial foods. The produce that we eat should be as natural as possible. The World Health Organization lists four of the most common chronic diseases to be cancer, diabetes, Chronic Obstructive Pulmonary Disease (COPD) and cardiovascular disease. They also indicate that an unhealthy diet with a high intake of sugar and carbs is one of the main causes of such diseases.

MENTAL HEALTH

There is a significant increase in mental health issues in our communities, much I believe to be as a result of the lives that we now live. Symptoms of mental health present themselves as a result of the imbalance in our lives and our adoption of a society that does not reflect our natural engineering. Generally, the strategy of Western medicine is to deal with and suppress the symptoms of disease through medication – or even surgery. Whereas traditional medicine disciplines, such as Ayurveda and Chinese medicine, explore the root cause of the problem behind the symptoms.

We are sold the idea that what we have and who we are in our naked skins isn't enough. We need to buy products to improve all areas of our lives. We then have to work harder to be able to buy these things that in many instances are detrimental to our health. No wonder we are stressed and unwell. Why is this so? Perhaps it is to serve the drug companies and the economy, as we know it? It certainly highlights the failings of the current system – something people have had a lot of time to think about during the COVID lockdown.

DRUGS AND ALCOHOL

When the world around you seems to offer no hope, finding an escape from your current reality is often an easy option. Escapism isn't just found in narcotics or illegal substances, it can be achieved through all manner of vices. However, drugs and alcohol are the most harmful to us physically. If we lack or don't form an environment that has solid foundations, our lives can seem futile, making it easy and appealing to turn towards vices that offer a way out. A sad example of this is the story of the lost generation of Australian Aboriginals, whereby they took a generation out, away from their parents, and put them in white families or boarding schools. They did this so that their native teachings, skills and traditions couldn't be passed down to the next generation. They wanted to wipe out their history and their very DNA, and as a result we can now see the negative impact this has had on Aboriginal society in Australia. What was once a vibrant and thriving community has now been ravished by its inhabitants turning to drink and drugs, as they cannot survive and flourish within a Western society, because it is does not allow them to live a traditional life – they cannot be who they are.

My Learning

I believe that understanding the importance of these connections has allowed me to remove the cover story that I'd been sold. Upon exploration, upon discovery and understanding the power that comes when developing these unique relationships, you begin to start to form a new paradigm. You see life as we know it for what it is. You realise that's not the way you want to live. You start to form a new direction and begin to build a new world where you're happier. You work toward something with deeper meaning and purpose.

A better connection with nature, each other and the metaphysical gives life more meaning. We've all read those interviews with famous people who have experienced fame and fortune, yet say that they can be in a room with hundreds of people with everyone knowing their name, yet they feel alone. Why? It is because they have yet to establish the true connections that I have shared with you. All that they experience is artificial, because they're not forming true relationships that feed the soul. Before I embarked on my Success Rebellion journey, I lacked purpose, and my life had no real meaning other than the attainment of material possessions. With this newfound connection and understanding, I now have clarity on my purpose and my connection with all things, which in turn has propelled me forward towards achieving success on a magnitude I could have never previously dreamt of.

Summary

It is vital to your Success Rebellion to understand the connection between you and the universal life force, and the impact it has on your life and the world around you.

Even small, almost insignificant actions can have a much larger impact on us and our world. Because of this, there are three key areas where you need to make your connection stronger – with nature, with each other and the metaphysical.

By understanding this disconnect and actively seeking to reconnect in these three areas you will have the skills and knowledge needed to lead the life you want to live.

Reflection

- Sit, stand or lie where you are and take a look around you. What do you see? How separated are you from nature? Has the modern world eroded your connection with the natural one?
- How could you begin to rebuild your connection with nature?

CHAPTER 8

The Power of the Plan

If until now your goals and dreams have eluded you, then I have good news. It's not that your desire for more was undeserved, nor that dreams of happiness or success are beyond you, it is simply that the plan you forged to attain your goals is flawed, or even more likely, that you failed to create a plan in the first place. Hopefully, as you've made your way through this book, you'll have begun to make changes and perhaps your beliefs have already shifted for the better. This chapter will help give a massive boost to all that you want to do to change your life.

Abraham Lincoln famously said, 'The easiest way to predict your future is to create it'. Now, of course, you could decide to hedge your bets and wait for good fortune to come your way, but how well has that worked for you up until now? Can you really afford to allow another period of precious life to pass you by? Now that you've been blessed with the understanding of what has been holding you back, you can no longer hide behind the excuse of ignorance, nor seek pity from those around you, as you've been granted an opportunity through the knowledge passed on to you via this book. Those who create a life according to their will do so not through sheer luck but as a result of establishing an action plan that directs them towards their goal.

Why You Need a Plan

Many of us were destined for greatness but sadly remain unfulfilled. We are provided daily with inspiration and ideas that will enable us to forge a new life. However, we often fail to act upon them. The very thing we've asked for has been given, but fear, procrastination and self-doubt ensure that they remain as just ideas. The answers to our prayers are often delivered in forms that aren't instantly recognisable. There is an expectancy that we will receive the very thing we have asked for in its full glory, giftwrapped, delivered by UPS. But this is not how the universe works. Very often it is for us to implement the force of action after we've had an inspired thought or idea. We have to recognise the signs and act upon the opportunity.

This is how the game changers do it. They reframe the way in which they perceive the world, see the opportunities as opposed to the problems, identify the missing links and capitalise where they can, and fill the void with their solutions. Many see but many stumble at the doing, held back by their limiting beliefs. Let's end that here and now.

Every journey starts with the first step, and as small as it may be, simply doing one small act that will take you forward is a win. It is then for you to build upon that with a second step, then a third, and before you know it, you're sprinting towards the finishing line. I've been there, and I know it can be hard to gain the momentum to get started, but once you do, there will be no stopping you. Over time, it then becomes a part of who you are, your default setting. You become a doer. Once you make the transition, you learn that nothing can stop you from creating the life you choose. No dream is too big or too outrageous for you to achieve. Following the wise words of Shakespeare in *As You Like It*, 'you realise that the world is but a stage', onto which you have become the main player, making your mark as you choose. The doer's mindset is geared towards acting upon their inspired thoughts and not allowing doubt to sway them from the goal.

Everyone has the ability to acquire this mindset, but the first step must be taken. It is up to you to first map out your journey, creating the chart that will guide you towards your new chosen life. Once the navigational map has been formed, it's time to release the anchor and move away from the comfort of the shore. No more discussions, debating and unnecessary prolonging. Now is the time for you to begin your initiation and move forth in the true essence of success, the journey!

Although we tend to fixate on the end game, it's your journey that yields true success. It is children, love, companionship, family and the many unique experiences they bring that really make our journey and forever impress upon the soul.

The child within us dreams of adventure, gripped by the excitement that comes from the unknown, but as we get older our youthfulness fades and so too does the naive courage that blesses us as children. We must remember to recognise the wants and needs of our inner child who is very much alive within us all. As children, we were a source of energy, full of life, operating on impulse. As soon as a thought popped into our head, we sprang into action before we could decide if it was a good idea or not. It's this natural impulse to act that has been lost. At times it may have resulted in us getting into trouble, but this is what it is to be young and to be a doer, before rational thinking subdues our natural spirit. You must once again become reconnected with your child genius, unafraid of the consequence of failing. Being impulsive is a gift, and by learning to hear its call, you tap into the invisible realm that can and will take you to heights that you cannot possibly imagine. Release the fears that hold you back and keep you from what you deserve. Miracles won't occur from calculated steps, strategic plans and formulated plots alone. The greatest success stories come about as a result of throwing caution to the wind and taking that leap of faith into the unknown, stepping out on the ledge knowing that you'll be carried.

These are the actions of the visionaries and the greats who have stood tall throughout time. Each of them knew this and embedded this principle into their daily lives. Intent alone will simply create dreams, but action turns these dreams into reality. Action is the physical ingredient required to create what you desire. Your acts, in conjunction with your goals, are necessary to achieve your desired results. Many have the best of intent and the grandest of goals, but do very little to make them a reality.

But action without a plan is not enough. And so on the flip side, we see people who have an outstanding work rate and are full of action, but their actions are not planned and so will not take them in the direction of their dreams. Or sadder still, they have given up on their dreams. This is the reality of many people. Going around in circles, paddling with a single oar, not taking the time to understand why they are not getting ahead, despite seeing others sail on by.

If something isn't working and you aren't where you want to be, then it's time to reassess your plan. If it's not working, it doesn't mean the game is over; it just means you have to learn to be a better player, and the first step in doing so is forming the plan that will guarantee you the win!

Cultivating the Right Habits

You may hear the word *ritual* and think of something dark, a satanic type gathering of hooded men and women chanting whilst standing inside a ring of fire. You've seen the movies, right? This is a misunderstanding of what a ritual involves. By definition, a ritual is a series of actions that are always performed in the same way and really bears no resemblance to the common misconception.

A ritual is simply an action or type of behaviour that you carry out regularly. We already perform rituals in some form or another each and every day. The act of washing your hands after you go to the toilet, eating around the table with your family at dinner or the act of prayer before going to bed. These simple acts have been accepted as a part of normal life and are, in fact, all forms of ritual that are now considered normal. They can sometimes be passed down through tradition, religion or social practises, but until now you've probably never thought twice about their origins and why you do these things. Take, for example, the act of saying 'bless you' after someone sneezes. This ritual is thought to have originated from the first-ever plague that weakened the Christian Roman Empire. It was believed that the sneeze was an early warning sign of the plague, and the pope of that time, Pope Gregory the Great, ordered all Christians to give this blessing if those who were in their company sneezed, and the ritual of saying 'God bless you' was formed.

Why is this important? Because unknowingly, you already subscribe to a set of rituals. Now the rituals I describe above are not harmful; my point is that we perform rituals unconsciously, often without first evaluating the impact they could potentially have on our life. This can dramatically affect your future goals and happiness. It can be the smallest thing but at the same time can be the very one thing that's holding you back from greatness. You goal may be to lose weight, but you have a ritual of having dessert after dinner or drinking soft drinks with lunch. Or maybe you want to learn another language, but you subscribe to watching three hours of TV an evening once the kids have gone to bed. You have to assess your daily rituals, and if they do not serve the future you, then it's time to make changes and define a new set of rituals that will take you where you want to be.

Rituals are the tools that allow you to direct the purpose of your life. They enable you to lock in behaviour as well as anchor in an emotional state with them. They are also an exercise that will help you develop the habits necessary for your success.

The mindset of elite performers rarely differs regardless of their field. They have all developed a set of rituals that enhance their beliefs and their ability to perform. Sports stars are known for their chosen rituals, such as having a lucky pair of boots or wearing a particular armband or item they consider good luck. These are all rituals that affect their inner beliefs and impact their energy states before game time. I am living proof that the development of a few key rituals can dramatically change our circumstances forever. From the moment I wake, I am locked into a set of rituals that immediately cultivates a way of being that is geared towards success. What I eat, how I eat, what time I wake, my training regime, my meditation practice, my commute, what I listen to, the information I consume, my media usage and how I structure my day are all examples of a conscious ritual process that ensures I am fully primed to becoming the very best version of myself.

Your morning is by far the most crucial part, as this sets the tone for the remainder of that day, which in turn impacts the results of your week, month and then your year. Developing the correct set of morning rituals will start to create positive change within your life that is noticeable within just a few days. The correct habits will provide you with total clarity, enhance your productivity and dramatically increase the impact that you make.

What I'm sharing with you isn't new – the knowledge has been around for the millennia – but it has been lost or forgotten. We are now moving into a new era of consciousness where we are waking to this lost knowledge, and understanding, and reclaiming practices that uplifted the lives of those who use the teachings in their daily practice and have transformed their lives forever. Knowledge is power but only when it is correctly used, so to truly reap the benefits if this wisdom, you must begin to introduce what I have shared with you here into your daily life.

Your goal from here must be to develop your potential. You have so much more to offer the world than you have previously been led to believe. By first defining your set of rituals and then through your practice, you can begin working from the ground up to build the behaviours, mindset, beliefs and habits that will start releasing your true potential and along with it a bigger and brighter future.

The Goal Versus the Plan

Firstly, a goal and a plan are not one and the same. Your plan is the route map that takes you towards your vision, with your goals acting as the route markers along the way. Your plan will highlight your chosen route that will take you to your end destination, your vision. It becomes the strategy that you will implement to get there. It will serve as a guide, holding you to account to your actions. If you should ever fall off track and lose your way, it's the point of reference that will help you to reconfigure the correct path back to where you need to be.

Your plan should highlight all that is required to fulfil your mission. It should include the skills and tools you must attain in order to accomplish your goals. For example, my vision for the future is to launch Yoko, a wellness-resort concept that will transform wellness, teaching some of what I've shared with you in this book, plus so much more. Yoko is a resort geared towards personal transformation for anyone wishing to tap into their innermost potential and live in alignment with their natural self through the sharing of ancient and indigenous knowledge. This is my purpose; everything I have experienced, learned and desired has brought me to this point.

To fulfil this ambition I had to grow and define who I had to become. I had to identify the skills I needed, how to build my personal brand and position myself as a business authority so that investors would take me seriously. I had to further develop my expertise on company branding, identify who I would partner with, source service partners that were aligned with my vision and values, do market research, learn about financial deal structures, build a community and identify growth marketing strategies. It was a mammoth task! By gathering this information I was then able create a plan, breaking my goals down into achievable chunks. I explain the full story of this Success Rebellion journey, which I am still on, at the end of this book.

By following this process, I grew into the person I needed to be in order to fulfil my goal. By creating an action plan, setting your goals and committing to developing yourself, you in turn can then become who you need to be in order to make your dreams and aspirations come true.

One of the key benefits of having a plan is being able to see your milestones. We can have a million ideas, but it's not until we get them onto paper that we can truly assess the quality of those ideas. The road to success can sometimes cause us to run away with ourselves. We can become so immersed in the process that we lose sight of the world around us and, on occasions, can neglect other aspects of our lives that we value. Being able to consciously plan a road map allows you to set goals for all areas of your life, creating balance ensuring all aspects of life receive an uplift.

Not So Smart

One of the key reasons for writing this book is to help you to move away from limitation and for you to see and become open to new possibilities. However, the traditional method of linear goal setting creates a blinkered approach that runs the risk of you missing out on the opportunities that would take you beyond that which you originally intended. This linear goal-setting approach serves a purpose but not in the new world I am proposing for you. We are creating a new life of freedom, so we don't want to work against that by setting goals that restrict your possibilities.

If you set a goal that has limits, you block other opportunities that may come your way. You have to have a degree of open-mindedness and flexibility. The purpose of a goal is to keep you on track, encourage action and let you know when you are winning. But so many adopt an overly disciplined tunnel-vision approach that sucks the fun and excitement from life.

Goals are a tool created to help you achieve success, but they do not represent success itself, so you must be able to differentiate the two. If you only measure your success based upon your goals, then you may be setting yourself up for failure. Take a flexible approach to reaching your goal. Don't write one that puts boundaries around you and creates tunnel vision. You want to create flexibility, so that if you see a new route, you can take it and go after that new opportunity. Very often, if something doesn't work out, it's because something bigger and better is waiting for you; therefore taking a step back and allowing the future to unfold will yield so much more than trying to force your desired outcome. (You'll see how this worked for me when you come to my latest Success Rebellion that at the time of writing is still a work in progress.)

To some extent, you have to learn to surf the flow of life, having dreams, seeing goals and then pushing the button that sets them on their way while not trying to interfere with their course of action. It's a balancing act that once mastered, will place you amongst the stars that shine brightest in this world.

The knowledge I share here will help you move into this way of being and will facilitate the transformation for you, enabling you to become the very person you were born to be: someone of immense power, higher values and here to serve a greater purpose. For this, my friend, is where the true game changers live. This is what I call the **Success Rebellion**.

Summary

All successful people have lifted themselves out of the limits of their environment. They have set flexible goals to help them become the person they want to be in life. Taking one step at a time, they moved slowly towards their dreams.

They took on a doer's mindset, always pushing fear to one side, never allowing negative emotions to stop them achieving success.

They got rid of rituals that no longer served their purpose and set about creating new rituals that helped them become the person they wanted to be.

Finally, they created the plan that enabled them to achieve their goals.

Reflection

Take some time to think about the following questions:

- Where does your road map lead you?
- What rituals do you subscribe to without truly knowing why?
- What are the habits that hold you back?
- And what are the positive habits that take you forward?
- Who do you need to become in order to achieve your vision?

SUMMARY

Success is, in essence, whatever you chose it to be. At the point where you stop comparing your life to the idea of what others believe success to be and define success on your own terms, the easier it becomes for you to achieve your happiness. In the past we may have allowed others to determine the course of our lives without giving consideration to how we genuinely feel about our reality and if we are living a life that makes us happy.

As we come to the end of this part of our journey together, I hope you are feeling inspired to take action to create the life you want to live and deserve to have. I have shared eight profound principles that form part of the **Success Rebellion**; so let's recap what has been shared, so that you can remain clear on how to create your successful future.

1. **Self-governance is about reclaiming control of your life.** No longer can you give excuses or blame others for your predicament. This is about stepping into the driver's seat and taking charge of your life.
2. **Environment: Where you live and hang out can set you up for**

failure or propel you towards your goals and success. Think about your surrounding environment, your influences and the information you consume. All of these can either elevate or hold you back from achieving success.

3. **Discovering your path: Your story can give you the competitive advantage in life** so long as you face your fears and follow the opportunities the universe has created for you.
4. **Vision: Your current reality is where you happen to be right now; it isn't a reflection of who you are.** It's up to you now to form a new outlook, a new vision of what you want your life to be. By forming a clear vision, you'll be able to define and describe the ideal scenario you want to imprint upon the world.
5. **Values: To move towards your vision you must first define who you are and decide on what you value as being important in your life.** You can create a vision, but unless it's reflected in your values, you're never going to achieve the happiness and fulfilment that you seek.
6. **Beliefs: If you believe something to be true then so, it is.** Your beliefs are what drive your behaviour and shape your view of the world and what is and what isn't possible. But to do this you have to begin to introduce a new way of thinking, a new way of believing, letting go of the old in order to move into the life that you deserve.
7. **Connection:** In order for you to move forward, you must understand how your relationships with nature, other people and the metaphysical directly impact you on a physical, mental and spiritual level.
8. **The power of the plan: Replace old rituals that hold you, and create new ones that empower you instead.** Then set your goal to change your life to become the person you want to be.

The illusion and the model of the life we have inherited are breaking down. More and more people are questioning their circumstances, waking with a knowing that this life they are living isn't how life is supposed to be. Let this be your wake-up call to a new day, one that empowers you across these eight essential principles that when applied to your life will begin not only to change your circumstances for the better but also spread to those around you, uplifting the ones you love and holding them close. Success is a gift to be shared with everyone and anyone whom you connect with, hence my inspiration for writing this book. It is my belief that everyone has the right to happiness and a greater quality of life. You too are deserving of all the good that this world offers. No longer do you need to accept anything less. As I have moved away from lack, negativity and fear, so you too can make the choices that will set you on your way to building a new life. You can become that person who excites and inspires those who watch your journey and to whom others look to for proof that it can be done.

Now that you've invested the time reading this book I really want you to benefit from its teachings by taking the necessary action. I hope this book has inspired and encouraged you to make choices that are outside of the scope of your normal day-to-day activities. This book has to be about creating change, not just reading about it. Consequently, the first step is to do something different, whatever it may be, and then to slowly build upon that. Use this book as a tool, not just to entertain you for the number of hours that you read it, but to be a catalyst for transformation, to bring you closer to your new life. With the right application and commitment in implementing the eight success principles in this book, you will learn that anything is possible when you become open to all of the opportunities around you.

It has been great helping you to get started on your **Success Rebellion** journey. If you've been inspired by this book and know a friend, family member or even a colleague who you believe would benefit from the book, I encourage you to take the first step towards being of service by gifting this book to that person. Don't worry, it's okay, you won't be without a book yourself.

By going onto the website www.ryanjackson.org/free and submitting the email address of just three people you feel will also benefit from this knowledge, you will receive a free e-book copy of *The Success Rebellion* for you to then keep, along with bonus material including *The 12 Disciplines of Success* e-book, transcripts and videos from interviews that I've held with some of the world's top self-help gurus during the research stage of this book.

I'm here to help you on your journey, so be sure to follow or contact me across any of the following social platforms:

Website: www.ryanjackson.org
Instagram: https://www.instagram.com/thesuccessrebellion/?hl=en
Linkedin: www.linkedin.com/in/ryanjacksonuk

Twitter: https://twitter.com/thesuccessrebel
Facebook: https://www.facebook.com/thesuccessrebellion

Thank you for investing your time with me in this book; I truly hope that it has helped you in some way to create a new perspective for your future. But before I go, let me tell you a little about my latest **Success Rebellion** and how I applied these principles myself.

BEFORE YOU CLOSE THE BOOK / BEFORE I SAY GOODBYE

My journey doesn't stop there, and it hasn't ended. The **Success Rebellion** never ends! I'd like to introduce Yoko, the latest project in my **Success Rebellion** journey.

Whenever I start something new I always start with waking up to what's required of me, and of course I maintain the self-governance needed to keep me on track.

Two years ago, my organisation, Gemini, had grown to a point where we were really making a difference in our industry, as well as to our local community through various social enterprise initiatives and donations. We have also empowered our people and our teams by helping them on their journey of professional and personal development.

I'm really proud of what we have achieved, but I have known since the beginning of my **Success Rebellion** journey that there is a lot more in me. This is a place that you may come to on your own **Success Rebellion** journey, or perhaps you already recognise it. However much I achieved with Gemini, there came a point where there was safety within what I was doing; it was comfortable, but on reflection I knew that continuing to do what I'd always done would inevitably bring about the same results I'd always had. I have always felt as though I must **step onto a bigger stage,** as I have a lot more to offer the world. And that point felt like it was the right time. But what did I want to do next?

Back to my dreams. I'd always had a dream of living in a tropical climate, somewhere that would allow me to live my life to the full, a place that fits with who I truly am. I could see myself living somewhere near the sea, living a more relaxed slower-paced life where the focus is on quality of life, not quantity, and much less emphasis on consumer goods. But unless I took new and deliberate – and also pretty massive –action, I was never going to get to that point. So what were my options? Well, I could sit and wait for an opportunity to occur or I could create that opportunity myself.

With a strong vision in place, my next step was to create a vehicle that would bring about this new lifestyle. I had to take the bull by the horns and make a commitment to making my dream happen. The idea of living abroad in a tropical climate coupled with the idea of taking the global stage in order to impact humanity in a bigger way was not going to remain just a dream; I was going to make it a reality. And so began the idea of Yoko, which would became my focus from then on.

Where did I get the idea? People often ask me this. To be honest, the answer is that it was just a small thing at first. The vision for Yoko first started as just a tiny idea from a holiday in Turkey. We stayed in a really lovely small boutique hotel of about twenty rooms, with lovely people running it. I looked around and said to myself, I can see myself having a hotel of some sort in the future. I didn't know when, there was no date on it, but that seed of an idea stuck with me. And I felt as though having a hotel one day would be a part of my journey and my experience.

All my holidays from then on were further steps in this new **Success**

Rebellion project. Whenever we stayed in a hotel, my wife and I always chose boutique hotels. We are not really into large complexes; it has always been quaint boutique or rustic-type hotels for us, and I knew that my future hotel would have the same feel. I didn't know how it was going to happen or when it was going to happen, and I didn't need to yet. I was happy to let it simmer away, giving it attention when I felt the time was right.

A further catalyst for this idea came about on a trip to Dubai for New Year's Eve. My friends go out there every year, so on this particular occasion we joined them. One evening my wife, Justine, was ill, so I took my eldest son, Raphael, who was just two at the time, to meet my friends at the Medina in downtown Dubai. We were sat at a restaurant that is towered over by the Burj Khalifa, which, with the lights and the light show they put on, is like a big Christmas tree – just wow, unbelievably beautiful.

My little one had gone to sleep in his buggy, so I could relax and enjoy a drink and take in the view. I was just lapping it up. I was transfixed by that building and was fascinated by whoever had had the idea of creating such an extravagant piece of architecture. Who was behind this amazing place? I wondered what they were like and what their background was. What inspired them to create this? And then the business questions started up: What was their financial situation? Then the life questions: What is the difference between this person and me? Why couldn't I do something like this?

I am not saying I heard a voice; it wasn't anything like that, but this idea came in a flash, that whoever they were, whatever their background or finances, I did know something about them. They had an idea, they had a vision AND they followed through and **took action**. And that was something I recognised. I smiled to myself, here we go, and it's just another **Success Rebellion. A dream, a vision, the right values in place, visualise where you want to be, make a plan,** make a start, and figure out the steps to get there. 'Wow', I thought, 'I know how to do this; if they can do it then why can't I?' There is no difference between me and that person; okay, they may be more connected, they may be more experienced, they may be wealthier, but I can build myself to that point. I know I can do that.

Now I am not saying I want to recreate the Burj Khalifa or something to that level of luxury and extravagance, but the seed of the idea of Yoko had always been there and now here was an extra spur. So, it was now more than a whim or a seed of an idea; my vision had grown, and I was now ready to move into, 'How do I begin to make this happen?'. And I made a commitment to myself then that as soon as I got home and started the New Year, I was going to get the ball rolling.

The Vision for Yoko

So the vision for Yoko has evolved over a period of time. In the beginning my thinking was that it was just a resort that reflected my wants and needs as an individual. Nothing more than, If I go on holiday, what sort of place would I like to stay at? What would I want?

And that's a great place to start, because any business that you create has to be a reflection of who you are. It has to reflect your inner values; it has to reflect your wants, your desires, and that's how you incorporate your passion into the project you are creating.

Initially, the plan was for a boutique hotel that offered a beach club. It would play a particular style of music; it would be a lot more conscious, a lot cooler than what was already on offer. And then what happened over a period of time through the conversations that I was having, was that particular things would really resonate with me and I would think 'Oh, that is what I have to do in the hotel'. It was like once my mind was open to this new project and my vision was strong, it began to filter, gather and attract ideas that strengthened my vision.

What I also found was that it was actually as a result of the challenges that I experienced along the journey to create Yoko that helped shape the concept and the end product. Here's an example: initially I intended to create my first Yoko resort in Thailand in Koh Samui. Unfortunately, there was a large stumbling block. As a non-Thai citizen, you can only own land if you get approval from the Thai Board of Investment (BOI), and then it has to be held within a company structure. In order to hold the land as a non-Thai entity you have to have over one hundred rooms, which wouldn't have worked, because it would have really diluted my concept, resulting in one of those big complexes that I didn't like. Or the other requirement was to have a capital investment of over five hundred million baht, not including land and working capital. And that is something in the region of about twenty million English pounds, which I didn't have.

So, this wasn't realistic, as it would take something very big for me to get to the point where I could secure that sort of investment. So I had to be practical, yet I didn't give up. What I discovered next was that if I was to create a resort that offered health rehabilitation, a wellness project, then that was something that the BOI would approve if they liked the idea.

So, then, this was the route I decided to take, and I tailored the concept to meet that requirement. So, the actual wellness concept wasn't in there at the start, but as it evolved, what became clear was that this was always what it was going to be. I just hadn't known it at the start, and it first came to me via an obstacle. So, I had the idea and the idea, grew and naturally evolved, but then the stumbling box of challenges helped me define what it should be.

What I love about this is that it feels like there isn't such a thing as a negative, there is only ever a positive, and the experiences that we might perceive as negative are often necessary for growth and opportunity. What started out as a barrier to my plans actually ended up giving me a unique niche for my resort.

Environment

As I have showed in Chapter 2, our environment is so important, and that is especially true for business. For Yoko, this is massively relevant, as there are specific places in this world that have a certain type of energy. And the energy of that location or that space attracts the energy of a very particular type of person.

You have what I refer to as the awakened slipstream, so for example, places such as Bali, Tulum, Thailand and Goa. And all these places attract a particular sort of individual, call them a hippy, call them an awakened traveller, call them whatever you wish. It is not just by chance that they are there, because it is the energies of these locations that call to that particular type of person. They feel drawn to these locations.

So, for Yoko, it was important for me to position the resort within one of these locations, where I could easily tap into those people on a similar wavelength. I'd considered Koh Samui and Koh Phangan but didn't find a strong enough community of conscious people there. And when the notion of Bali came up and I began to explore Bali and I discovered the people who gather there and the significance it has in relation to the earth's energy, I knew that this was the right spot, this was the environment that would be perfect. Not just for Yoko but perfect for me in order for me to become who I needed to be to build my tribe and build the community.

So my growth has continued, hand in hand with Yoko's, and in order for me to be the best version of myself and to better serve the community, it is imperative that I immerse myself in that environment and fully embrace that way of living. This is essential for me to evolve and to become who I was born to be.

Since leaving behind that weed-smoking, college drop-out life many years ago and starting my Success Rebellion, my life has been continuously evolving. And now I see that there are many more levels to go. Each time I want to get to the next level, I have to change my environment and immerse myself in a new lifestyle that is going to help me shed the limited identity that I had created for myself. Only then can I become the person that I always was, rather than being limited by the traits and different personality aspects I had adopted to survive in the culture and environment I had found myself in. Genuine progression – a **Success Rebellion** – requires forgetting our limited programming, ignoring the social pressures and just stripping away the façade to get back to our true nature.

Values

As I explained in Chapter 3, it is essential for us to know what our values are in order to know that each day we are turning up as the best versions of ourselves and we are living our life in accordance with that better version. Although I had designed my life to meet most of my needs and uphold my values, it wasn't 100 percent aligned, and I think one of the key values that was missing was being of service. And specifically how I could help others in a more impactful way beyond what I am already doing with Gemini. Yoko changed this for me.

Now I'm not a person who is going to go out on the road and feed a million homeless people, and I'm not a healer either. That's not where my skill sets lie, but I'm aware of what my natural skill sets are, who I am and what I'm capable of. And I know that I am capable of using my talents to build the hub, to create the location in which I can gather a community of like-minded individuals and help them in their awakening and in their growth, in their evolution and journey to enlightenment.

By developing Yoko, I will be able to positively impact the lives of others, inspiring them too shine their light, and that has a domino effect. My contribution is to house and create the community and help to build a tribe who can help elevate the consciousness of others. That awareness and growth will permeate through the community members and spread out into each and every one of their own communities. So that is my dream and now a solid aim with Yoko.

With Gemini there are a lot of responsibilities that shackle me, and so I first need to free myself from some of those day-to-day ties in order to move into a new direction to really commit myself to being of service in the way I feel I am supposed to. I'm sharing this with you so that you can understand that we never stop growing and that once you start, there'll always be a further **Success Rebellion** you can embark on.

Beliefs

A big challenge for me was being able to condition my thinking and my beliefs in order to make Yoko a reality. This was something that I needed to do on a daily basis.

One of the key things and the barriers to Yoko being built was the limit of my beliefs. We create according to who we are, and our beliefs are a fundamental part of that; they manifest our realities. There was still a challenge of unworthiness that I had to face, because I had not yet convinced myself I was worthy of achieving such a task. So I had to really go deep and convince myself, and I am going to call it this: I had to brainwash myself into believing that I was worthy.

I had to tell myself that I had already created it, that I was already there, that I had already achieved my goal, so that I could tap into that energy and incorporate it into my being. And I did that continuously until things started to evolve, and I will do it until it is completed. So, most evenings I would create time and space to sit down and visualise Yoko. I would visualise the resort being complete. It was just me there, and I visualised myself walking through the lobby, fully enjoying the feeling of, 'WOW, I did it; this is what I have created'. My vision connected and tapped into that immense feeling of reward and accomplishment to know that I had created something; I had created my dream.

I would walk around the resort enjoying how it looked and felt, breathing in the scent of jasmine and frangipani incense. Pausing by the lotus flowers blooming in the ponds, I enjoyed all the different areas I'd created. Next I'm centre stage where I am sharing my journey with guests, explaining the concept and the philosophy of Yoko. Underlining what we were there to do and how our mission is to help people with their awakening and support them with their growth and development as people.

That feeling of seeing my vision come to life was incredible, and so every night I would tap into this vision, so that it became embedded within my unconscious mind.

This is how a **Success Rebellion** works. An idea or an opportunity arises, and you take a first step and then another. You take action, and as you do, it then reinforces your vision, it reinforces that dream, and then it also reinforces your self-belief step by step. The more you believe, the more you create; the more you create, the more you believe. And so it becomes a perpetual cycle, and then as you strengthen that and believe in it, things start to manifest themselves further.

CONNECTION

This is probably one of the most important principles for a **Success Rebellion**. And that was reinforced for me when I was completing this book during lockdown. In that time I was able to further strengthen my connection with nature; it grounds me and takes me out of the head and into the heart. And by strengthening that connection and making that transition from the head, from out of the ego and into the heart, I strengthened the connection that I have with other people.

I started to dissolve the judgments that I have about life, about things, about people and formed genuine connections based on love. And I am not talking airy-fairy blah blah blah. I am talking about just being kind, being present, just being there and listening fully. And so strengthening those relationships with both nature and those around me strengthens my relationship with myself.

It brings me to a point where I know who I am, which strengthens my connection with the metaphysical, which then provides me with the guidance and the intuition and the inspiration to make the right decisions where they are necessary.

And so, for Yoko, when having conversations and negotiations with people about it, one of the key influences of the experience was to help reconnect through a state of nature. In order for me to do that, I had to really delve deeper into understanding indigenous coaches and their practices. Because they were far more connected to the cosmos and had a far greater understanding of their position and place here on earth, and even though we refer to them as being primitive, they were a lot more advanced and evolved than we are in that.

Strengthening my connection with nature provided further clarity on what I needed to do with Yoko. It guided me along the way. It provided subtle signs that I could follow. Everywhere I looked and listened I'd find inspiration for Yoko. I'd be in conversation about something random and think 'WOW, that needs to be a part of Yoko. I need to integrate that within the concept; I need to be able to share that with the Yoko tribe and the community. That would be amazing to help them reconnect and help to awaken them.'

All these different elements that are helping me build Yoko, I might have missed had I not been in tune. By developing your connection with the earth, with nature and people, you start to shift your awareness to your heart and away from the mind. The mind is where the judgment, the ego, the anxiety, the doubt, the worry, all live, but in the heart you have peace and knowing.

By keeping your awareness in the heart you connect with the divine, with the metaphysical, and so you know your truth and are able to establish what it is that you need to do to find support and guidance along the way.

By strengthening your connection with nature and by knowing your truth and who you really are, you begin to understand what does and does not serve you. This makes life so much easier, because it is like a gateway with an open door – it's clear that this is the route you should take. And also what you should not be doing – those things that take you away from your journey. It provides clarity and gives you a point of reference.

Connection is similar to **values** in a sense, as it begins to provide the foundation or the framework for your behaviour and how you should live your life in order to get the most from it. What connection does is guide you; it is the subtle signals and signs that highlight the way forward. So, at a point where you may not be sure of what is next, being grounded and connected works so that you recognise the truth when you see or hear it. Often you'll also get a clear message, such as 'I need to do that', or the opposite: 'actually, that does not work for me'.

Connection centres and grounds you and heightens your state of awareness, and you become more aware of your surroundings, more aware of your actions, more elevated and more conscious. It raises your vibration to see things as they really are.

So with Yoko, having become aware that this was to be a wellness concept, I then got the message that I wanted to stay away from a typical wellness concept where the focus is all about massage or detox. Because even though they do offer forms of healing, what I wanted to create was a place where people could awaken to do the inner work that needs to be done, bringing people back to a state of connection.

So, the programs that I intend to deliver are being designed to create that awakening within the guests, whereby subtle shifts in their state of being will bring them to a greater sense of consciousness. This is needed to 'feed' the individual, to feed the soul and to make up for the limitations of our education system, which sadly is still based on training us to be a part of the industrial revolution rather than equipping us for the information age.

The vision for Yoko is to elevate people to a higher state of being, so they are in the best possible place and living a life according to their destiny.

The work I am doing in preparation is strengthening my own connection and relationships. And becoming more heart-centred, allowing me to be more in flow and to know the moves I am supposed to make and those I'm not supposed to make. It made me more aware of who I am, and being more aware of who I am makes me more aware of my place within this world.

Discovering Your Path

To discover your true path, you need to own and not shy away from your story. For me, everything naturally fell into place once I began my **Success Rebellion**. I realised that I had to embrace everything I had been through in my life. Writing this book was a difficult yet necessary step on that path, because there are people, even my mum, who aren't aware of certain choices that I made in the past. But I decided that discovering my true path and creating a lasting **Success Rebellion** meant embracing who I was and not hiding from that.

We need honesty and to make the most of what we've been through, taking the golden nuggets from all of our experiences, the good and the bad. We should use that knowledge to help us throughout the remainder of our journey as well as use it to our competitive advantage. I also knew that my experiences would allow me to connect with a wider audience than you would typically see within the wellness and personal development scene.

My previous life experiences allow me to connect with people who may be unreachable to icons such as Tony Robbins and Oprah Winfrey. They speak in a way that is so different to how ordinary people speak and think, that it can create a barrier to what they are trying to teach and share.

I learned this during one of the turning points in my Yoko **Success Rebellion** when I attended a healing conference in Portugal. This was in the early days of having the idea for Yoko. I was very much out of my comfort zone, and it was a considerable investment for me to attend, but I knew I had to put myself in that environment in order to grow.

Given the nature of the event you might get an idea of what it was like. I call it the Oprah Winfrey culture, where everyone is full of love and light and they have adopted these particular ways of speaking, and if you are not that way then it may feel quite uncomfortable. It's like they speak another language, and I think this is where the disconnection with more everyday people occurs. And why they find it hard to reach those ordinary people not yet on the journey.

Even though I was out of my comfort zone, feeling I didn't belong in that community, I was conscious and understood everything that was spoken about. I felt a huge sense of contradiction, because though I didn't feel a part of that community, I knew I belonged there. I felt I was more aware spiritually than a lot of the individuals that attended, even though I didn't necessarily "look" or "sound" the part. It was pretty strange, I can tell you, but I knew by that point that growth isn't always comfortable or straightforward.

There were some amazing people in that room. I knew what distinguished me from everybody else in that room is that like Robbins and Oprah they would find it very difficult to connect with a lot of the people who would most benefit from the teachings that were being shared.

They would find it difficult to relate and difficult to connect, because the speakers didn't understand where those particular people – who are yet to begin their journey – are at. And so that gave me great perspective on what I was here to do, and although I felt a bit detached from that particular community in one sense, I knew I belonged there in another. And I knew that I would one day deserve to be on that stage sharing my philosophy of what I want to bring to the wellness industry.

It solidified my vision and path. It was necessary for me to understand the contrast of where I was and where the rest of the community was. I could see an opportunity and a need within the wellness industry that I was in a brilliant position to serve.

So that helped to solidify what I was here to do, my path and how

Yoko would help others and help the world by reaching out and creating a space and a communal concept where people could be themselves. And Yoko would help them do that in a way that didn't require signing up to the love and light approach, instead they could just be themselves.

Power of the Plan

When I first had the idea for Yoko, it felt like it was a million miles away from where I was. But it was never out of my reach. Yes it was a mammoth project, and given that my background wasn't hospitality or wellness, I had to be clear about my role in it. I was a qualified EFT practitioner, qualified NLP practitioner, and a qualified mindfulness coach but these were skills and qualifications that I had acquired over the years but had never really practiced to any great extent. I see now that this was all readying me for the overarching Yoko project, whereby I conceived of it, curated it and made it happen but didn't deliver the teaching.

Knowing that this was my next level **Success Rebellion** journey, I had to formulate an action plan, and the first stage of that was establishing what it would take to bring this to fruition. So, first identifying the magnitude of the task. This involved me speaking to the right people, firstly to architects and people on the ground in Bali. And of course facing the biggest challenge that most people are going to have in business, funding the project. You can speak to and get all the right people involved, but unfortunately what makes this world go round is money.

So, the biggest challenge I had was the financial aspect of it, because if I had access to the money, I would have completed Yoko already. And yet, would that have been the right thing, given how much my plans have changed? If I'd had the financing right away and it had been faster and easier, it may have turned out differently, into something I didn't really want. I may have ended up with a hotel without the wellness aspect, an aspect that has evolved into the most important detail of all. So anyway, the next step was to create a clear road map for what I needed to do in order to create the plan and secure the funding.

Meeting with and learning from people experienced in resorts and the logistics of setting up and building in Bali helped me establish a road map for Yoko. I started to formulate this into a plan, but that plan couldn't be rigid because so many things pop up unexpectedly, and as I've explained, my plans have evolved and changed many times, and I was cool with that. So the learning here is, you can't be rigid in thoughts, you have to be open to opportunity and open to ideas and let the time be right.

So having first established all the components of the project, from there you then define what it takes in order to make this happen, and you create a road map that you can break down into achievable goals and then into stages with their own timelines.

I've come to realise that what is especially important, is 'who' you need to be in order to make your vision real. And this is something that people often forget. They have a plan, and they take some action. But to really succeed on the journey you have to evolve to become that person who can make it happen. You need to grow to reach that stage where you make that final vision come alive. You have to identify the skills you need and answer a whole lot of questions. What qualifications do you need? What do you need to know? Who do you need to connect with? What sort of relationships do you need to develop?

In the beginning it can seem like a mammoth undertaking, but as with, you just break it down into sizeable, manageable chunks so that your actions can be done daily, weekly, monthly and beyond. And you know exactly where you are with things, and you'll get there by just managing that process and steadily working through it.

It doesn't happen overnight. Getting to the point I am now with

Yoko was approximately two years in the making. This involved creating a feasibility plan and a workable business plan and defining the concept fully. And I would say that I'm probably midproject because I'm continuously learning new things, acquiring new information. And so for your **Success Rebellion**, you have to be able to do the same: to chart a course of action but then to adapt and tweak and amend as you go along.

So then slowly and surely you will see your dreams start to become a reality. It will start to manifest, bit by bit, stage by stage, and then before you know it . . . Hey, presto – it begins to happen, and then it's just following that path to seeing it happen! So what next for Yoko? Watch this space.

And for your **Success Rebellion**: I wish you luck. Reclaim your future and embrace your **Success Rebellion,** and become who you were always intended to be.

Namaste,
Ryan Jackson

REFERENCES

Integrated chronic disease prevention and control, World Health Organisation website https://www.who.int/chp/about/integrated_cd/en/

W. David Myers, in Judy Mandell's article 'Why Do We Feel Compelled to Say "Bless You" When Someone Sneezes' (*New York Times*, 2019), https://www.nytimes.com/2019/09/17/well/mind/sneezing-sneezes-god-bless-you-manners-etiquette.html

Mark Bowden (2001) *Killing Pablo* / Grove Atlantic

Tony Robbins (1986) *Unlimited Power* / Ballantine Books

Tony Gaskins (2016) *The Dream Chaser* / John Wiley & Sons

Carmine Gallo (2016) *The Storytellers Secret* / Pan Macmillan

Esther Hicks / Jerry Hicks (2004) *Ask and It Is Given* / Hay House Inc

Bruce Lipton (2011) *The Biology of Belief* / Hay House UK

Daniel Goleman (1996) *Emotional Intelligence* / Bloomsbury Publishing PLC

Tony Hsieh (2010) *Delivering Happiness* / Business Plus

Hira Ratan (2014) *Sun Gazing: The Magical Key to Magical Abilities: Sun Eating*

FILMS

Benjamin Stewart (2008) *Esoteric Agenda*

Benjamin Stewart (2009) *Kymatica*

Discover the Gift (2010) Equilibrium Entertainment / Lightstone Entertainment

Tony Robbins: *I Am not Your Guru* (2016) Radica Media / Third Eye Motion Picture Company

INTERVIEWS

Dr John Demartini

Richard Bandler

Bruce Lipton

Patrick Wanis

PAGE V

https://bcorporation.uk/certification?gclid=EAIaIQobChMI9uno6uq_6AIVjLHtCh2fkQ3GEAAYASAAEgInU_D_BwE

PAGE 23

https://www.brainyquote.com/quotes/maya_angelou_634505

PAGE 34

https://www.business.com/articles/10-principles-of-success-quotes-to-inspire-from-jim-rohn/

PAGE 40

https://www.ncbi.nlm.nih.gov/pmc/articles/PMC2527715/

https://bmcpsychiatry.biomedcentral.com/articles/10.1186/s12888-016-0794-9

http://med.stanford.edu/content/dam/sm/parkerlab/documents/Yuen_JPsychiatricResearch_04.2014.pdf

PAGE 42

https://globalhealing.com/natural-health/health-benefits-of-sungazing/

https://medium.com/@GeosafeUSA/why-i-stopped-wearing-sunglasses-f1116384c36c

https://articles.mercola.com/sites/articles/archive/2019/11/02/sunglasses-and-eye-health.asp

PAGE 51
https://www.hsph.harvard.edu/nutritionsource/vitamin-d/

PAGE 54
https://museeyslparis.com/en/stories/les-annees-dior-1-1

https://www.cnbc.com/2017/09/11/why-you-should-find-a-great-mentor-if-you-want-to-be-successful.html

https://www.dreamteamfc.com/c/archives/uncategorized/184878/alex-ferguson-cristiano-ronaldo/

PAGE 59
https://en.wikipedia.org/wiki/Taj_Mahal

PAGE 62
https://medium.com/@GeosafeUSA/why-i-stopped-wearing-sunglasses-f1116384c36c

https://articles.mercola.com/sites/articles/archive/2013/09/16/sunglasses-myths.aspx?v=1600701296

PAGE 66
https://www.huffingtonpost.co.uk/adrian-griffiths/the-best-way-to-predict-yb17654468.html

ACKNOWLEDGEMENTS

I believe this to be an extremely powerful book that has the ability to change lives through the philosophy it shares. I couldn't have written it without the valuable help and support of a number of people.

A very special thank you must be given to Dr Richard Bandler, Patrick Wanis, Dr John Demartini and Bruce Lipton, who shared their time, allowing me to interview them in the research stages of this book.

A big thank you also goes to Jacq Burns, whose guidance helped me to shape the book into what it is now – and at the point when I was done, pushed me to do that little bit extra, which has made a big difference in the final read.

I'd also like to thank Linda Innes, who has supported me over the past few years on various projects and whose influence has helped me to become a better writer.

Last but not least, I'd like to thank my beautiful wife, Justine, who has always believed and supported me in the pursuit of my dreams. Also, Raphael and Remy, my two gorgeous boys who inspire me each and

every day to be a better person and create a legacy they will be proud of.

For those who have also helped me along the way in the creation of this book and have not been mentioned – thank you!

ABOUT THE AUTHOR

Ryan Jackson is the founder and CEO of Gemini Parking Solutions, the UK's only "values-based" car park management company. A serial entrepreneur, Ryan's passion is to build disruptive companies that shake up the status quo and pave the way for a new age of thinking in various industry sectors.

Over the past fifteen years, Ryan has been committed to raising his standards, becoming the best version of himself through personal and spiritual development, the results of which have manifested in multiple businesses in the UK and abroad.

In 2012, Ryan founded Gemini Parking Solutions. Entering an industry with a notorious reputation, Gemini sparked the positive change that the car park management sector desperately needed. Gemini raised standards to unprecedented heights and became the benchmark for quality. Boasting some of the best qualitative statistics in the parking industry, with a distinct and unique company culture that empowers employees on all levels, Gemini continues to grow, develop and improve.

His vision is to uplift his team, clients and his wider community by sharing the success principles that have allowed him to build his own successful life.

As a successful entrepreneur and mentor, Ryan is keen to share his expertise and knowledge in order to better serve society and help others to create remarkable lives allowing them to truly express themselves from a place of abundance and wellbeing.

Printed in Great Britain
by Amazon

49389273R00098